W9-AJP-717

DATE DUE

The Lambs
of Libertyville

The Lambs
of Libertyville

◆ A Working Community ◆
of Retarded Adults

◆

TIM UNSWORTH
Foreword by Betty Ford

CB
CONTEMPORARY
BOOKS
CHICAGO

Library of Congress Cataloging-in-Publication Data

Unsworth, Tim.
    The Lambs of Libertyville / Tim Unsworth ; foreword by Betty
Ford.
       p.   cm.
     ISBN 0-8092-4178-1 (cloth) : $17.95
     1. Mental retardation facilities—Illinois—Libertyville—Case
studies.   2. Mentally handicapped—Illinois—Libertyville—Case
studies.   3. Terese, Robert.   4. Owen, Corinne.   I. Title.
HV3006.I3U57   1990
362.3'685'0977321—dc20   90-43788
                                        CIP

Published by Contemporary Books, Inc.
180 North Michigan Avenue, Chicago, Illinois 60601
Manufactured in the United States of America
International Standard Book Number: 0-8092-4178-1

To the Lambs of Libertyville,
who give back far more than
they receive.

To Corinne Owen and Bob Terese,
who have fed the Lambs for
over thirty years.

To Jean, who energized this book
as she does my life.

The Lambs provides a unique and deeply caring program which has touched and changed hundreds of lives. You have my sincere congratulations for the work you do. Through the training and career opportunities provided, the Lambs enables special people to live independent lives.

—Betty Ford

Betty Ford is no stranger to the Lambs. On March 12, 1976, the then–First Lady presided over the dedication of the Lambs' first residence, now called the Intermediate Care Center. She returned again on September 9, 1980, to cut the ribbon for the opening of the Country Inn restaurant. On that occasion, the gracious former First Lady acted as hostess. She worked with the Lambs themselves, greeting and seating other friends of the Lambs. In 1986, only a serious back ailment kept her from being the honored speaker at the Good Shepherd Award Dinner. On several occasions, she has welcomed Bob Terese and Corinne Owen, founders of the Lambs Farm, to her California retirement home. Betty Ford remains an honorary board member of the Lambs Farm.

Contents

Preface

In mid-1989, Bob Terese and Corinne Owen approached a mutual friend, Harvey Plotnick, and suggested a book about retarded adults. Specifically, they wanted to tell the story of the Lambs Farm, located in Libertyville, Illinois, about forty miles from downtown Chicago. Plotnick, president of Contemporary Books, contacted me and suggested that it was a worthwhile story to tell. After only one visit with Bob and Corinne, I agreed to write *The Lambs of Libertyville*.

This is the story of two people who had a dream and determination. Out of a conviction that retarded adults can lead satisfying lives and that, far from being a burden on society, they can contribute to it, Bob and Corinne founded the Lambs Farm, a not-for-profit organization that would become one of the premier facilities for developmentally disabled people in the United States.

The Lambs of Libertyville is not intended as a definitive text. It is simply an informal history of the growth of a community. It is hoped that people who have an interest in mental retardation, which touches virtually every family in America, will find useful lessons and emotional support.

I am grateful to Corinne Owen and Bob Terese, who patiently answered hundreds of questions during over fifty hours of separate interviews. The staff of the Lambs Farm were remarkable for their openness and cooperation. They are as unaffected and honest as the Lambs themselves. The members of the Lambs' community became instant friends during the months of visiting at the Farm. I will never be the same.

Harvey Plotnick took a personal interest in this book. His suggestions were invariably on target. Mark McMahon, another friend of the Lambs, contributed the beautiful cover art. My wife, Jean, became as involved in the story as I did. She often accompanied me to Libertyville and read every word of the drafts. I owe them all more than I can tell.

The Lambs
of Libertyville

Toward Understanding Special People

The Lambs Farm attracts some 300,000 visitors each year. Many of them have never been face to face with a retarded person. The experience forces them to confront their own fears and insecurities. Once they have been exposed, their thinking changes. No one comes away from the Lambs unaffected.

At first, however, many normal people don't quite know what to say.

Brian has Down's syndrome—a genetic accident that results from an additional chromosome in female egg cells and male sperm cells. Down's syndrome children, perhaps the most recognized of the retarded community, have upward-slanting eyes and puffy eyelids. Sometimes their tongue protrudes slightly and their ears are abnormally shaped and set low. Down's children can be happy, active participants in family life because they are responsive, loving, and even-tempered. And they have a sense of humor.

Brian's father, a retired fire fighter, loves to golf and has taught Brian the game. When Brian's father introduced him to some fellow golfers, one of them asked nervously, "Oh, you play golf. That's great. What's your handicap?"

"I'm retarded," Brian answered.

The Lambs of Libertyville is about hundreds of adults like Brian. They are American citizens of every race, creed, and

1

color. At present, the Lambs range in age from twenty-one to sixty-five and are about equally divided between men and women. Not all have Brian's sense of humor, but on balance they laugh more than they cry. About half have physical problems, and some have emotional problems. Most have brothers and sisters who live in the "normal" world. They visit their families often. Many have been part of the wedding party at family weddings—bridesmaids and best men to brothers and sisters who love them and feel no need to hide them in the family closet.

"We're just a little slow," one Lamb said. "We just need more time to catch on." But for too many years, it wasn't that way. The acceptance wasn't there. The concept of retarded adults working in a business, especially one that dealt directly with the public, was light-years away.

An estimated ten million Americans are mentally handicapped. Their lives take them down many paths. For some there is home, but home is often a struggle against loneliness and long hours with nothing to do. For others there may be work at one of the few sheltered workshops. But here, too, the specter of loneliness appears in the day-in-and-day-out monotonous tasks. Finally, there is the cruelest path of all: an institution where there is no struggle at all—only existence.

For a small group of mentally handicapped young adults who were to become members of the first Lambs' community, there was a new path to walk—one that offered hope instead of despair, happiness instead of frustration. This new way led to the Lambs Farm, an idea that began simply back in 1961, the idea for an atmosphere in which retarded youth could grow and be accepted, the idea of a business attended by young people.

Armed with little more than determination, Bob Terese and Corinne Owen fought great odds to turn a belief into a reality—a belief rejected by many others in the field of mental retardation.

They began with a pet store on Chicago's Near North Side. Nursed along by Corinne and Bob and a handful of parents and friends, the Lambs Pet Store became a self-supporting business, employing twenty young adults, in only four years.

To make room for the growing number of young adults, the Lambs Farm needed more facilities. After years of careful saving, plus an interest-free loan from friend W. Clement Stone, the Lambs purchased a fifty-one-acre farm near suburban Libertyville, Illinois. Here, the young people could have more opportunity, more jobs to learn, more things to talk about, more chance for social growth.

"What we wanted to accomplish was to give the adult retarded a sense of accomplishment, a sense of performance," Bob Terese said. "But more important than that, we were taking the fear out of life—and fear is the most crippling handicap to retarded as well as nonretarded."

The road to Libertyville was not an easy one for Bob and Corinne. They were rejected by the professional and academic communities, viewed as visionaries and ideologues, called religious fanatics, and accused of taking advantage of the developmentally disabled. But they refused to abandon their belief that the mentally retarded can function in a complex society and lead more fulfilling personal lives.

"I think we saw the Lambs Farm as an ideal society," Corinne Owen said. "We believed we could create an ideal society, one that would offer a workday, something to come home to, and a full social life. We could be a model not only for mental retardation but for institutions that are housing the blind or the physically handicapped or the aged."

The designation *Lambs* has caused a few to bristle. At a time when "normalization" is the new cliché, "Lambs" suggests a patronizing approach. The name is actually the brainchild of Bob Terese, who thought of it almost on the eve of the opening of their State Street pet store in 1962. It comes from the scriptural passage of St. John (21:15) in which Christ orders his disciples, "Feed my lambs." The name has now become synonymous with the institution's mission.

After thirty years, the Lambs Farm is no longer freestanding. While it remains private, it is a fully accredited institution visited by professionals from all over the world and serves as a training center for the Department of Rehabilitation Services.

Who are the mentally retarded? Simply stated, a mentally retarded person is an individual of subnormal intelligence, one who is slow to reason and limited in his or her capacity for learning. In this century, the intelligence quotient, or IQ, is used to measure an individual's mental capacity. The highest score is 200; those scoring in the lower range from 0 to 70 are considered retarded. However, mental retardation is more than just a score on a test. Further, IQ results are no longer thought to be unchanging, nor are they the sole measure of ability.

At the Lambs Farm, the mean IQ is about 50. However, the IQ is now only one index of an individual Lamb's profile. Some Lambs are simply slow learners with related physical complications. Others may still need occasional help with dressing.

At one time, applicants were as young as sixteen. Today, because the State of Illinois now funds education for the retarded from ages five through twenty-one, the admissions team at the Lambs Farm encourages applicants to take full advantage of that education before coming to the Farm. The average age of the present community is thirty-five.

The American Association for Mental Deficiency defines mental retardation as "subaverage, general intellectual functioning which originates during the developmental period (conception to 17 years) and is associated with impairment in adaptive behavior." The cause may be known, but more often it is not. It may be a hereditary condition, or it may be an unfortunate accident of nature. It can occur within a wide range of severity. It cannot be cured in the usual sense, but its effects can often be minimized.

Retardation is thought to be permanent and irreversible. A retarded person is wholly rational and, in most cases, is capable of understanding the nature of his or her disability.

For centuries, the retarded were victims of the law of the survival of the fittest. Retarded children—half of them also suffering from physical handicaps—usually died in infancy. Infanticide was common among primitive tribes and even during sophisticated Roman and Grecian empires. If these people were not destroyed by their own citizens, conquering tribes or armies often slaughtered all of the aged, infirm, and handicapped.

In medieval times, the retarded were sometimes kept at royal courts and used as jesters or simply "pets." They were often objects of ridicule. They were thought to bring good fortune to their owners. Lacking this dubious privilege, many were consigned to be the village idiot.

Given the tragic mixture of superstition, medical and scientific ignorance, and some very bad theology, the retarded were often considered to be possessed by evil spirits. As early as Old Testament times and as recently as the colonial period in America, the retarded were viewed as witches or warlocks and were often put to death.

The practice of killing the physically or mentally afflicted was not limited to ancient times. As recently as the Nazi regime in Germany, Hitler's followers did away with any malformed child in an effort to create the "super race." Today, modern scientific knowledge provides a procedure known as amniocentesis, which can detect certain fetal disorders, including some forms of mental retardation, and allow the prospective parents to terminate a pregnancy.

In the largely agrarian society of an earlier time, retarded children could be kept on the farm and trained to do tasks. In the extended families common in those days, grandparents, maiden aunts, and bachelor uncles could often help care for a retarded child, thus easing the parents' burden. During times of slavery, the wealthier families could assign a slave to care for the retarded child.

With the advent of the industrial revolution and the rush to the cities, retarded citizens suffered greatly—and in silence. Early hospitals for the retarded were shared by the mentally ill. Retarded children were often bound to walls or chairs in unheated cells and fed much like swine.

In his essay on the origins of intelligence, psychologist

James C. Dobson cites an early work by Dr. Henry Goddard, which, unfortunately, misled and confused nearly two generations of behavioral scientists. In his 1914 text, *Feeble Mindedness: Its Causes and Consequences*, Goddard concludes, "Normal intelligence seems to be unit character and transmitted in true Mendelian fashion." With this statement, Goddard established the pervasive belief in "fixed intelligence"—a term that meant that intelligence is an innate dimension, which unfolds only as a person matures physically. Reduced to its simplest terms, it meant that one's genetic endowment is fixed and that environment is of no significance in the development of cognitive ability.

This belief marred all education, but especially the education of the retarded. Writing in *The Mentally Retarded Child and His Family*, Dobson observes, "All intellectually defective children were believed to have inherited an inferior quality of genes, or perhaps they were damaged during the pre-natal period."

For too many years, all the retarded were lumped into one subhuman group, considered untreatable and untrainable. Experts ignored the fact that there are many levels of retardation, ranging from the mild to the severe. The prevailing belief, firmly held, was that retarded children can never be anything different from what they are—or that they can never produce any type of offspring other than their own type. Based on that misconception, retarded females are still sterilized in parts of the United States.

For years, the denial of the possibility that the retarded can be trained seemed to be the one intractable, pathetic, and pitiful exception to the otherwise triumphant advance of modern medicine. Further, other societal ills were firmly attached to the retarded. Even the high-functioning retarded were regarded as menaces to society. In 1915, readers of *Good Housekeeping* magazine were told that the retarded "are born of and will breed nothing but defective stock. From this class seven-eighths of our criminals are recruited. Take care of the morons and crime will take care of itself. . . . They are awkward, grotesque and clumsy and their foolish speeches provoke only ridicule, mockery and jeers." *Good Housekeeping*'s firm recommendation was to remove them from society.

Society has changed substantially since 1915, but as recently as 1989, two adult men were executed although it had been firmly established that both were retarded. The view of the retarded as criminals may stem from the fact that some 45 percent of prison inmates have tested as mildly retarded in the so-called "dull–normal" range. Books recommending institutionalization as the best treatment for a retarded child remain on the shelves in medical libraries.

Translated into practice, this attitude meant that retarded children would receive little more than custodial care. As a result, in a very real sense, they grew even "more retarded."

For generations, the higher-functioning retarded person was simply referred to as "feebleminded." Around 1910, the American Association for the Study of the Feeble Minded elected to term this group "morons." The word derives from the Greek word for fool, and morons were considered just competent enough to pass for fair imitations of normal people, although their mental development ceased somewhere between the normal equivalent ages of eight through twelve. Morons could develop, but their progress was slower. To the untrained eye, they could talk the same way as anybody else as long as the conversation didn't get too complicated, and they could even jog along after a fashion for several grades in school, learning to read and write and do simple sums.

Not many years ago, the majority of the members of the Lambs' community were classed as feebleminded, a term now regarded as being as derisive as "cripple" for the physically handicapped. However, negative terms are no longer used, and no single retarded person is lumped into a single group.

Descriptive language—even clinical, professional parlance—always runs the risk of over- or underdescribing individuals. The most common word used at the Lambs Farm is *retarded*. It appears on the Farm's stationery and in its literature. "Our special people must know who they are," Bob Terese said. "Their condition cannot be masked with language. Once people accept this fact, progress can be made."

Because of that preference, the preferred word for this history of the Lambs Farm is *retarded*. Other terms include *mentally disabled*, *special-needs people*, *mentally handicapped*, and *developmentally disabled*. None of the descriptions are meant to demean or patronize. The Lambs themselves prefer the designation *Lambs*, and when one employee was asked about terminology, she answered, "We don't call them anything. They're just people."

Like normal people in society at large, the Lambs are treated as individuals and are educated to tasks that are equal to their ability. A visitor to the Lambs Farm would have little difficulty identifying many of the retarded, partly because some have physical handicaps. On the other hand, many high-functioning members betray few signs of their disability. Many can read and write and have excellent—sometimes uncanny—recall. Further, because they are mentally, not emotionally, retarded, their unvarnished and unfiltered charm often masks certain learning difficulties.

Retardation occurs in three out of every hundred births, according to Dr. Richard Koch, director of the Child Development Division at Children's Hospital in Los Angeles and professor of pediatrics at the University of Southern California School of Medicine. In *Understanding the Mentally Retarded Child: A New Approach*, Koch and his wife, Kathryn Jean, wrote about many of the fears that infect families touched by retardation. Parents feel guilty about having produced such a child. They may blame each other. Their pride gets wounded. They ask bitter questions: "Why did this happen to us?" "Is it hereditary?" "How long will he or she live?" The financial burden of raising a retarded child often strains the marital relationship and the relationships with other children. One mother of a severely retarded young man observed, "It either makes or breaks a family."

Fortunately, the situation continues to change for the

better. Researchers are continuing to investigate the causes of retardation. Experts can now evaluate many of the disorders. Institutions resembling huge holding pens have been closed. The retarded now live in homes, small institutions, group homes such as the Lambs' homes, and even in private residences, apart from any institutional setting.

Attitudes toward the retarded continue to improve. After years of secrecy, America's most famous family, the Kennedys, told the world of their sister's condition. As president, the late John F. Kennedy established the President's Panel on Mental Retardation, a twenty-one-member group of professionals in the field. From it has emerged significant legislation benefiting the retarded.

In 1968, the assembly of the International League of Societies for the Mentally Handicapped adopted a bill of rights for the handicapped, which was adopted by the United Nations. It proclaims "All of the human family, without distinction of any kind, have equal and inalienable rights of human dignity and freedom." These rights include the right to medical care, to physical restoration, and to such education, training, rehabilitation, and guidance as will enable each person to develop as fully as possible. The resolution goes on to embrace not only educational activities but also those that will enable the retarded to participate in all aspects of community life. "Above all," the resolution ends, "the mentally retarded person has the right to respect."

In recent years, public understanding has been raised considerably by highly publicized events such as the Special Olympics. More recently, the enormously influential television industry has introduced retarded roles into some of its dramas. The first, a professional actor playing the role of a retarded person in the cast of a popular law drama, did a great deal to place the retarded within a positive framework in society. Later, another retarded character was introduced—this one played by an actress who is mentally retarded. In 1989, a family series was introduced with a young, retarded actor in a leading role. Such portrayals are viewed by millions, and with each exposure, the perception improves.

The Lambs of Libertyville is the story of one approach to the treatment of the developmentally disabled. There are others, equally valid. The genius of the Lambs Farm's approach is its simplicity and directness. It is an idea born of two people who share these same qualities.

◆ Chapter 1 ◆

The Founders

"Our people would be great with preschoolers. We could have a day-care center here that would attract kids from all over the area. And we've got to think about a retirement home for our residents. They're getting along in years."

Bob Terese was thinking out loud. At one level, he knows that a day-care center partly staffed by retarded adults isn't a reality. He knows that state regulations require that day-care center workers be high school graduates and meet certain other criteria. But that doesn't water the spark inside him. He's been up that road before. "Some day," he said. "Some day it will happen."

Bob Terese is as ordinary looking as a post office clerk. He is the man in the white coat who comes out when one rings the bell at the supermarket meat counter. He could pass for an insurance salesman or a bartender. He is everyman. It doesn't matter to him. Bob Terese cares little about appearances or pedigrees.

Bob is 5′9″ and soft where older men tend to get soft. He is an indifferent dresser, favoring casual polyester and soft-soled shoes. He wears a suit when he has to but has managed to get through life without a tuxedo. He has a mild speech impediment that emerges when he is excited. Asked about it, he will tell that he has stuttered all his life—and that is that. It is just one of the things he accepts in himself, as he

11

accepts so much in others. Bob Terese doesn't mark anybody's paper.

He was born at Luther Memorial Hospital in Chicago on May 12, 1924. His Italian-American mother was Angela Casella, one of twelve children, eleven of them girls. His maternal grandfather was Anthony Casella, who had come to America from Italy to live with his sister and her husband and who had been apprenticed to a barber. His father, Charles Terese, was from a family of five children, born and raised in Chicago to Joseph Terese, an Italian immigrant.

Grandfather Casella hated barbering. He marched to the beat of a different drummer—a trait that would emerge in his grandson. While a teenager, Anthony hopped a freight with a friend and headed west. Near Dubuque, they came upon a monastery of Trappist monks, a group known for their strict rule and warm hospitality. His friend returned to Chicago, but Anthony stayed at the monastery.

At seventeen, he announced that he wanted to enter the Trappist Order, but the wise monks thought this an appropriate time for him to return to Chicago and to test the world outside the monastery. "It was a good move," Bob Terese observed more than a century later. "If my grandfather hadn't returned to Chicago and met my grandmother, there may not have been a Lambs Farm, and I would not have returned to the abbey at New Melleray to buy honey for our shop at the Lambs Farm."

Angela Casella and Charles Terese were married in the early 1920s. They moved to the Austin neighborhood of Chicago, opened a mom-and-pop grocery at the corner of Division and Massasoit, and—just a few years before Bob and his brother, Russell, were born—purchased a home on Massasoit Avenue, just three blocks from the store.

The Terese boys would take the traditional path through school, although Bob found formal schooling very difficult. In a world of right-or-wrong answers, Bob was a dreamer. Russell completed degrees at De Paul and Loyola universities and became a successful dentist, practicing until his death in 1973.

Bob Terese's early years were, in his words, "a normal, happy childhood." He spent a great deal of time at his grandmother's home in Chicago's Logan Square neighborhood. Although he had only one brother, his mother's ten sisters, one of whom was only two years older than he, were more like siblings than aunts.

Life was that of a traditional, working class, ethnic family. As soon as he was old enough, he helped out in the grocery store. These were the worst years of the Great Depression, but there was always food on the table. "Eating wasn't a problem," Bob recalls. "Paying the mortgage was."

Bob received an uneventful, traditional Catholic education at his parish elementary school, St. Angela's, and later at Fenwick High School in Oak Park. Fenwick is a highly touted private high school, conducted by the Dominican Fathers. Bob was not uncomfortable there, but the scholastic approach to education was not suited to his romantic mind. "I liked history and literature and religion," he said. "The other subjects didn't appeal to me." However, the Fenwick years were pleasant ones. He was a good athlete who enjoyed the playing more than the competition. In 1942, after four years of daydreaming, Bob graduated near the bottom of his class.

A few months after high school, Bob enlisted in the U.S. Navy. It was during the height of World War II, and he was quickly shipped to the Pacific theater, where he would witness the fighting at Iwo Jima, Okinawa, and the Philippines. He was assigned to a cargo ship, one that occasionally carried troops.

He had asked for duty on deck. He wanted to see the sun and the sky. But it also made him a witness to some of the tragedies of war. "It was unreal," he recalled. "I was on deck, eating a peanut butter and jelly sandwich and watching men get into those landing crafts. Then they came back, badly wounded. Some died, and I recall the burials at sea with the flag, the salute, and then the splash of their bodies as they hit the water. It was sad."

The war years were an extension of his high school experience. Young people simply went along in those days. Life's issues were clear. One rarely questioned. Bob eased some of the painfully dull hours by playing poker. He was good at it and even better at sending his winnings home. Out of his seaman's pay of barely $100 per month—and the earnings from the card games—he was able to save $5,000, a nest egg for a very uncertain future. Years later he would joke, "The war was good to me. I traveled the world and saw a lot of places. I didn't shoot anybody, and nobody shot me."

In 1946 he mustered out at the naval base at Treasure Island near San Francisco and headed home.

Once home, the veteran found life closing in. He realized that he had virtually no goals. He knew only that he could not work in a factory and that he dreaded the thought of being trapped in an office. It seemed to him that all of his friends knew what they wanted to be and he didn't. "My brother knew that he wanted to be a dentist and went right to it. I didn't know what to do. I only knew that I didn't want to be trapped."

Bob took the same route as thousands of other veterans took. He used his GI Bill, a veterans' benefit program, to enroll at Chicago's De Paul University. He was buying time.

Bob enrolled at De Paul in the hope that he would discover a vocation that he would find satisfying. He tried business courses and detested them. He lasted about eighteen months at De Paul's downtown campus on Lake Street, then transferred to its Lincoln Park campus on Fullerton Avenue. The latter campus, on the North Side of Chicago, provided a more traditional preparation in the liberal arts and teacher training.

He enrolled in the physical education program. He was a decent athlete, and he enjoyed the program, although he had no idea what he would do with an education degree. He also knew that he didn't like the program enough to make it a career. After four years of courses in commerce and physical education, Bob had learned only one thing: he could not endure routine and dreaded being tied down. "We never heard of the term in those days," he said, "but I guess you could say that I had the personality of an entrepreneur, although I didn't know it at the time."

He left De Paul just a few credits short of his degree. "I finally convinced myself that I couldn't march around that gym one more time," he recalled. "So, I marched out." Years later, much to his pride and amusement, De Paul would honor him as one of its outstanding alumni.

It was 1950. Bob was twenty-six years old and recently married. He had met Mary Ruth Miller on a blind date. Although she lived only two blocks from the Terese family, Bob had never spoken to her. Mary Ruth recalls, however, that a much younger Bob had knocked her off her bicycle when they were kids.

Bob and Mary Ruth had two children—Michael, born in 1951, and Carol, born in 1953. After a few meaningless interim jobs, including one as a playground supervisor for the Chicago Park District, he learned that the Milwaukee Road railroad had an opening for a fireman-engineer and that the position paid more than a teaching position. "These were diesel trains, so they didn't take much work," he recalled later. "My biggest job was to keep the engineer awake."

Early in their marriage, the Tereses purchased an old home in Wood Dale, Illinois, and began the task of rehabbing it. Bob's hours on the Milwaukee Road were from midnight until 8:00 A.M., so he found time during the day for the rehabbing work.

The railroad job put food on the table, but it was terribly boring. In an effort to find something more meaningful, Bob investigated the possibility of selling insurance. Urged on by Ray Talmadge, a friend he had met at church, Bob took two days of aptitude tests. The tests revealed that he was, in his own words, "either too dumb or too honest." So he stayed with the railroad.

With the birth of Michael and Carol, however, the need for additional money caused him to stop by a gas station not far from his railroad job in Bensenville to ask about the possibility of part-time work as an attendant. The station owner didn't need anyone, but Bob left his name, just in case.

What followed might have been sheer happenstance. Bob, a deeply spiritual man, sees it differently. There have been too many similar experiences in his life to explain them away as the luck of the draw. He clearly sees the hand of God in these casual happenings.

The day after he left his name with the station owner, a man named Bert Fisher came in for a fillup. Fisher had never been to the station before. He told the station owner that he was the parent of a retarded child and that he and some other parents were attempting to organize a parent-operated school for the retarded in Glen Ellyn, Illinois. The school needed a part-time bus driver. Fisher took Bob's number and called him. The hours were perfect; Bob accepted the position over the phone.

In September 1957, Bob Terese, who had never been aware of seeing a retarded child, became a part-time bus driver at the Bonaparte School.

On October 14, 1971, while Corinne Owen was returning home after a day at the Lambs Farm, the car in which she was a passenger was involved in a serious accident near St. Mary's Road and Route 176 in Libertyville, Illinois. A witness to the accident, Dolly Galter, called the police and informed them that there was at least one fatality. Corinne had suffered a severe head injury and a number of lesser hurts that caused Dolly Galter to believe she was dead. Coincidentally, Mrs. Galter was a close friend of Corinne's. She and her husband, Jack, were and remain major benefactors of the Lambs Farm, having provided the funds to renovate the old barn that is now the pet shop and to buy supplies for the fledgling restaurant.

Although badly injured, Corinne Owen survived. "She's tougher than Bob," observed one of her admiring fellow workers. Indeed, those who have come to know Corinne Owen have found that the soft-spoken, 4'11" minister's daughter, who thought she would spend her life teaching music, has a piece of steel in her that may have held the Lambs Farm together through some of its most troubled days.

After months of recuperation, Corinne Owen returned to her office in the Founders' Building at the Farm. The accident has aggravated a back condition and caused mild memory loss. Dates and events have become a bit jumbled. But names are etched in her memory—especially those of the members of the Lambs Farm community and its benefactors. More important, the light in Corinne Owen's heart shines as bright as ever. She is the North Star of the community.

Corinne Boren was born in Greenville, Ohio, in 1915. Her maternal grandfather had an eighty-acre farm in Arcanum, not far from Greenville, one that had been in the family for some years.

Corinne's father, Ezra Boren, was a farmer who would later bring the family to Chicago and become a part-time minister. Her mother, Hazel Fourman, was raised on a farm but had left home to attend college. Hazel liked the school but couldn't stand the boarding house cooking, so she returned to the farm.

Corinne's father was of Scotch-Irish descent; her mother's family roots were German. Ezra Boren's sister, Lola, was seeing a man about the same time as Ezra Boren was dating Hazel Fourman. In a move that must have shocked the local farm community, the two couples eloped and were married at a double wedding ceremony in another town.

Ezra and Hazel Boren returned to their farm near Arcanum, a short distance from the Indiana border. The Borens farmed one of five sections of the land owned by Corinne's maternal grandfather.

Their first child miscarried. Corinne was their second. Her younger sister, Dorothy, was born not long after. Following Dorothy's birth, Corinne's mother became very ill. Dorothy was moved to the home of an aunt, where she lived until Corinne was in the fourth or fifth grade. For Corinne, it meant a lonely, isolated life on a farm.

Her paternal grandfather, Timothy Boren, had died of

Huntington's chorea, a rare, inherited degenerative nerve disease that would later cause the deaths of Corinne's father and sister. Her grandmother had married again and lived in Greenville, not far from a favorite aunt, Hetie Martin, with whom Corinne spent many happy hours.

When Corinne was a child, her father had a religious experience, called "seeing the light." He and his family began attending a small church, something Corinne came to enjoy because it brought her in contact with other people. The days on the farm were happy ones but marred by a certain loneliness. "You could go weeks without seeing anyone outside the family," she recalled.

Corinne attended a one-room school for three years. It was a long walk to the school, and her only companion was a boy she "couldn't stand." But the school was fun, in spite of the rote learning and the gnawing poverty of some of her classmates. "We weren't really poor," she said. "After all, we lived on a farm. My mother canned a lot. But there wasn't much luxury." Corinne often took additional food to school to feed her classmates.

When Corinne was barely out of third grade, her father decided to give up farming and become a minister. However, Ezra Boren had only a high school education and needed to find a college to begin his preparation. He sold everything on the farm and moved the family to Grundy Center, Iowa, where his brother, Emory, had a restaurant. Corinne and her parents moved to a single partitioned room above the restaurant and shared a bathroom with the restaurant's customers. Hazel Boren became the cashier and waitress while her husband began his studies.

Corinne enrolled in the town school. It was small, she remembers, but "it had grades in it"—a big difference from the one-room schoolhouse in Ohio. She loved the companionship and was obviously loved in return.

In the mid-1920s, Ezra Boren enrolled in the Moody Bible Institute and moved the family to Chicago. The family found a modest flat near Kedzie Avenue and Madison Street. The communal toilet was down the hall, and Hazel Boren had only a gas burner on which to cook. However, after three years of Uncle Emory's restaurant meals, Corinne was delighted to eat home cooking.

Corinne enrolled in the Beidler Elementary School on Walnut Street. "There were so many kids there that it was frightening at first," she recalled. In just over three years, she completed four years of elementary school. It was during this period that her grandmother came to visit from Ohio with Corinne's sister, Dorothy. Her mother would not let Dorothy return, and at last Corinne had a sister.

In the early 1930s, she entered John Marshall High School. It was a huge high school, its corridors and classrooms crowded with noisy students. For tiny, sensitive Corinne, the four years at Marshall were not overwhelmingly happy ones. She made only two real friends. With one exception, she liked her teachers, but she recalls only one teacher who had a genuine impact on her.

Money remained a serious problem. Her father continued his studies at the Moody Bible Institute by day; at night he worked as an elevator operator at a luxury apartment building at Seventy East Walton Place on Chicago's Gold Coast. He got little sleep—sometimes only three hours—but continued his studies through Moody and matriculated at the Northern Baptist Seminary. Her mother worked as a waitress at the Marshall Field's department store on State Street.

Corinne worked two summers at a hot dog stand at a Sears, Roebuck department store. It was hard work, involving twelve-hour shifts at least two days each week. However, the food was free, and Corinne earned enough to buy her first pair of silk stockings—a must for a young woman entering college.

In spite of the tight family economy, Corinne managed to dress well and to make plans for college. Her clothes were often passed on to her through the wealthy residents of the Seventy East Walton building. Her grandmother, a skilled seamstress, had come to live with the family. She and Corinne's mother were able to tailor the gift clothing for Corinne.

She majored in what was then called public school music (music education today). Corinne liked music; the family had a piano and had scraped pennies together to provide her with occasional lessons.

She loved North Park College. It was a school she could get her arms around. The school of music was located in a simple home on the campus. The teachers were caring and competent, especially her piano teacher, who introduced her to the Robyn Method of teaching piano.

In the 1930s, teachers with a new method of training musicians often gave free weekend workshops to prospective teachers. Corinne attended many of them at the Lyon & Healy music store in Chicago's Loop, absorbing a wide variety of teaching techniques.

Still essentially shy, she made few friends at North Park, partly because as a commuting student she could not avail herself of the fellowship offered at the college. She earned modest amounts baby-sitting and as a telephone-answering aide for a physician who lived at Seventy East Walton.

Even before she left North Park College, she began giving private piano lessons in students' homes. While a student at North Park College, she practice-taught at St. Patrick's Academy and St. Francis School, and she was later hired by St. Thomas Aquinas School. Soon she was spending three full days teaching in various parts of the city.

Except for her brief employment at St. Thomas Aquinas, she never taught full-time in any school system. The private lessons often occupied her six days each week in a wide variety of homes. She charged $1 per lesson but often took less to accommodate people who could not afford that amount.

In the Hyde Park neighborhood, home to the famous University of Chicago, she gave lessons to a community of Filipino children whom other teachers would not accept because of their nationality. Such prejudice did not even register on Corinne's heart. "They were my best students," she recalled. "They were so talented and so bright."

Two of her favorite students were Fred and Rudy Vergera. Fred Vergera, now an engineer with Steel Joist Fabricator Co. in Chicago Heights, recalls meeting Corinne in 1939. She taught Fred and his brother, Rudy, now an engineer living in Charleston, North Carolina, at their home and later at a studio she had rented at the Lyon & Healy Building. The lessons continued for six or seven years; the friendship has endured for over a half-century.

Corinne met her husband, Trevor Owen, through his sister and her church. He had left school to help support a large family, which was in difficult circumstances following the death of his mother. Trevor worked as an elevator operator and later for Sprague-Warner Foods, distributors of a gourmet line of canned goods.

Following their marriage in 1938, Trevor and Corinne purchased a duplex home in Blue Island, Illinois, which they shared with Corinne's parents. Their first child, Bette Lynn—now Bette Ireland—was born a year later. Two more children followed: Doris, now Doris Servey of Decatur, Illinois, and Victor, now a businessman in multimedia in Elgin, Illinois.

When Corinne's parents decided to sell their share of the two-family home, the Owens opted to build a home in West Chicago. Trevor, who was now a manufacturer's representative, found the property while en route to Elgin and, later, found a housing plan in a magazine. He built their home from scratch.

Corinne had set aside her teaching career to raise their three children, but when Victor entered nursery school, she became a part-time salesperson for a successful reading program called Childcraft. Sales were slow at first, but within a few weeks Corinne was averaging seven sales for every ten calls. It was a talent that would serve her well as a fund-raiser in the years that followed at the Lambs Farm. "At first, I didn't even tell Trevor," she said. "But when the commissions began to arrive, the income proved a blessing. It paid the children's way through private schools and put custom cabinets in the kitchen."

The sales of the reading program and, later, of subscriptions to *Life* magazine provided her with part-time employment until she met Bob Terese.

It happened this way: Corinne's territory for the Child-craft reading program extended throughout Wheaton and St. Charles. After a few years, she had mined the territory as much as possible. She was looking for another challenge. One day, in conversation with her friend Jean Adams, she heard about Jean's work with retarded adults. She knew nothing about the retarded, but when she heard that they were being taught the basics of cooking and music, she thought, "I can do that."

Not long after, Jean Adams informed her that she would be leaving her job to prepare for her third child. It was one year after Bob Terese had taken his bus-driving job. When Jean left to have her baby, Corinne Owen signed on at the Bonaparte School as a teacher.

Although Bob and Corinne attended the same church, they did not know each other. Their link was Jean Adams, a fellow church member. Since meeting, the two had become more tightly bound by their shared interest in the welfare of the Lambs and in their deeply held religious beliefs.

The Lambs Farm remains politely and firmly nonsectar-ian—not irreligious but respectful of all expressions of faith. "Our name may have Christian roots," Bob Terese wrote in 1970, "but our program is open to everyone. We wouldn't be Christian if we weren't."

Over the years, students from Protestant and Catholic seminaries have volunteered at the Lambs Farm. Church groups have availed themselves of the facilities of the Country Inn, and Jewish organizations have provided energetic and tangible support.

"Corinne and I both feel that the Lambs [Farm] is an answer to prayer," Bob wrote in 1970. But their religion is not exclusive. It is a religion of love.

Their faith remains the heart of the Lambs' community today.

◆ Interlude ◆
Karl Menninger, M.D.

"I remember the day very well, now a long time ago, when a young man and a young woman, two friends with a common, unselfish purpose, came to see me in my Chicago office."

The late Karl Menninger, perhaps this country's best-known psychiatrist, was then consulting at the Stone-Brandel Center in Chicago. He wasn't particularly anxious to have Bob Terese and Corinne Owen call on him. Public figures such as Menninger are understandably cautious. They are frequently called upon to endorse projects that range from the visionary to the totally unstable. Menninger listened attentively but cautiously.

"They were too warm-hearted, too earnest, too eager on doing something about the . . . people who seemed to count as nobodies," he wrote in a 1989 letter to the Lambs Farm. "Corinne and Bob were concerned about the handicapped which even some of the most philanthropic people were overlooking."

Dr. Menninger was still cautious when he agreed to visit the Lambs Farm, then not nearly as developed as it is today. As Bob Terese recalls, the eminent psychiatrist appeared somewhat irritated by the intrusion. It was a long ride to Libertyville, and Bob and Corinne clearly were hopeful of his approval. He wasn't certain of what he would find.

They were seeking his endorsement because their entire

philosophy was under question. Bob and Corinne were a threat to the established public agencies and even to the private institutions that provided custodial care for those wealthy enough to afford it. A thumbs-up from the distinguished author and founder of the Menninger Clinic would open doors and muffle the criticism from others.

"It's great. I will help in any way I can," he said after his visit. "Anyone you talk to will want to join you, for you are very convincing, the need you represent is very compelling, and the tenderness and intelligence you show is persuasive."

Some time after his initial visit, a member of the Lambs Farm staff interviewed Dr. Menninger at his office at the Menninger Foundation in Topeka, Kansas. Here are some excerpts from that interview:

> Wonderful, if anyone has the patience to do it. All other approaches are approaches of neglect. . . . I think the mentally retarded so often has either a totally lacking or else a very low self-image. Just think how much having a job or having something to do, having something which one is depended upon for doing . . . think what that does! . . . Everybody's happy when they see these supposedly hopeless, useless people doing something beautiful, interesting and energetic. . . . It's just an inspiring sight to walk through that place.
>
> People say they love little children. Ah, the little children! They mean the cute ones, the charming ones. Sometimes children aren't cute and aren't so obedient or so bright and so attractive. Who loves them? Who cares for them?
>
> They believe it can be done. They start out with a belief this can be done. Somebody tries. Somebody loves these children. They're lovable people. People can be lovable even if their face isn't pretty. Those who do the caring need what they're getting out of it. If somebody wants to put their life into it, to put their love into it, this is a way of showing that you care.

On the use of animals in working with the mentally retarded, Menninger said, "That's one of the great features of the place. I think that's wonderful. Think how much animals mean to people who don't have as many human contacts.

"I like that metaphor—the Lambs. I just love the Lambs, that's all."

Dr. Karl Menninger was an honorary board member of the Lambs Farm and the recipient of its Good Shepherd Award. He died July 18, 1990.

♦ Chapter 2 ♦

The Bonaparte School

Another bus driver for the young people at the Bonaparte School showed Bob Terese around. In a matter of hours, Bob decided that the job was not for him. For appearances' sake, he would keep the job a week.

"One hyperactive boy was yelling bloody murder at nothing in particular," Bob said. "Another, whose beard had just started to grow, was slobbering onto his jacket. Some were simply rocking back and forth on their seats to silent rhythms of their own; others were huddled speechless and motionless against the bus windows, like puppets whose strings had been cut."

Bob was neither a social snob nor an intellectual elitist, but these young people were an affront even to his accepting disposition. He would quit as soon as possible.

He told the parents' representative to find another driver. The money for home renovation could wait. These young people seared his emotions and churned his stomach.

By the end of the first week, the desperate parents still had no one to take Bob's place. However, in that same period, he had started to see his charges differently. He began to see the little smile on their sometimes distorted faces and to acknowledge the wave of the hand when they got on the bus. "I began to see them for what they were: nice kids who were simply different," he recalled. "I was receiving my first education in special education."

He decided to stay.

What happened to Bob Terese would happen to uncounted thousands of other people who came to know the Lambs in the years ahead. The Lambs have become missionaries for the retarded. They are not hidden behind fences or seen at a distance, walking two abreast from one institutional building to another. The Lambs invite visitors. Residents walk freely around the campuslike property just off the Illinois Tollway. Visitors are greeted by warm, trusting adult retardees, going to and from their jobs.

When the Lambs greet the public, they break down walls of fear inside the minds of people brainwashed by the distorted expectations of a self-absorbed society. When people first experience the retarded, they respond much as Bob Terese did. However, after just a little exposure, the curtains of fear and prejudice are parted. In smaller but significant ways, Bob Terese's initial experience is echoed every day at the Lambs Farm.

The Bonaparte School was just one of a number of small, independent schools for the mentally retarded in the greater Chicago area. Virtually all were owned and operated by the parents of the retarded. As recently as 1957, local school boards made no provision for educating the mentally handicapped. The school system provided driver education and swimming pools for those sound of mind and body, but parents of the retarded were entirely on their own, although they were expected to pay taxes in order to ensure the education of normal children. Of course, there were state institutions—warehouses for the physically and mentally handicapped. However, with good reason, most parents considered such places to be a last resort. Conditions at maximum security prisons were often better than at such centers.

The parent-supported schools were often forced to hire any person they could get to teach their children in any building they could find. It was a makeshift system of education, held together largely by the dedication and sacrifice of

caring parents. There were schools and homes for the retarded children of wealthy parents. These provided genteel
care and a modicum of learning for a few, at a price only a
few could afford.

The Bonaparte School in Glen Ellyn, Illinois, had been a
country school for farm children. It was built on a knoll just
behind the grounds of the beautiful Morton Arboretum, a
sylvan Garden of Eden that Bob and Corinne would use later
as a learning asset. Once a one-room schoolhouse, the building now contained two upstairs rooms with a third room and
kitchen in the basement. It had been empty for years; it was
drafty, and it leaked; rodents enjoyed almost unlimited access. The parents had wheedled the authorities to rent the
facility for a dollar per year.

When the students left the bus just before ten o'clock each
morning, they went to one of two classes: under fourteen
upstairs, over fourteen downstairs. For Bob, there was nothing to do for the next three hours but sit in his bus and read.
"I bore easily," he admitted. "So I started to observe the
older students' classes."

The sight was disheartening. The basement was just that, a
dull, dingy room. It wasn't dirty, just in need of freshening
up. The lighting was poor. Although the windows were
uncurtained, little natural light invaded. It was the kind of
space one stored things in.

The students were wandering about aimlessly. Some
simply crouched against the walls. Others sat in one-armed
desks, appropriate for note-taking in college. They did busywork, much of it meaningless to their situation.

Upstairs the younger children were taught by a Mrs. Kopecky, an energetic, receptive woman, bursting with ideas.
Downstairs, the teacher, who was nominally the principal,
would attempt to occupy the twenty to twenty-five students
with some task before rushing off to some administrative
work that often occupied her for most of the three-hour
school day. She had experience teaching normal students; she
provided a curriculum that might have made sense to normal
children but was completely inappropriate for the retarded.

More often than not, she left the class in the hands of one or two parent-volunteers, who did what they could to impart what the teacher thought they should be learning.

These were not uncaring or insensitive teachers and volunteers. They must be understood within the context of the times. In starting a private school for the retarded, these parents were attempting to break through barriers that were literally centuries old. The Bonaparte School would never have survived without the services contributed by these parents.

In selecting the material to be learned, the teachers were not unlike parents of normal children who spend hours teaching their children to count. As often as not, the child eventually memorizes the numerical chant without the least understanding of what the figures mean. It is intellectual fast food with little application to their lives.

So with these parents. "They learned to write [numbers], and they learned to recite them," Bob recalled, "but there weren't more than two in that group who, if asked, could have correctly counted out five objects." They knew the names and symbols, but taught this way, they would never comprehend their use. It was much the same with the alphabet. They copied letters and words. Most would never know what it all meant. A student might copy, "The cat is a dog," for all that it meant to him or her.

Parents of retarded children often want their special child to be "normal." As a result, with the best of intentions, they attempt to teach them what normal children might learn. (Ironically, it has been established that much of the rote material taught to normal students is meaningless. They often have to unlearn and relearn the material before they can genuinely understand it.)

The Bonaparte School looked like a school. It sounded like a school. If the teachers drilled hard enough, their young charges would have a semblance of normalcy. If a young man, for example, could recite the multiplication tables, he might gain a foothold in a society that had already rejected him. Such thinking would never really work, but it was the best that people knew how to do.

The basement classroom had a loom on which the students could weave. It worked very well for some but could accommodate only two students at a time, and it occupied the attention of one teacher. Besides, while some could weave, others would never learn. However, the students had been divided by age, not by ability levels. Thus, some learned while others simply vegetated.

More disheartening for Bob Terese was the sanding and lacquering of wooden plates. "At first, I thought this was great. They're doing something productive," he said. Then to his horror, he witnessed them sanding and then lacquering the same plate over and over until it was reduced almost to the size of a coin. It was busywork—a way of absorbing some of their adolescent energies.

Bob noted something else, however: these students actually enjoyed the sanding and lacquering. They worked carefully, almost meticulously, often applying eight or nine coats of lacquer. They were pleased even with the limited creativity of their work.

During the hours he observed the students, something else was happening to Bob Terese. The bus driver was becoming a teacher. Gradually, the students began to look at him, to make eye contact, to smile. Bob smiled back. One morning, a young Down's syndrome child threw his arms around him and said, "Good morning, Mr. Terese!" Unwittingly, Bob had been absorbing the kind of love that only the retarded can give. He still had many questions and no answers, but he was hooked.

Like the parents of the retarded, Bob Terese had no special skills and even fewer insights. He was still in good condition physically, and he had heard the boys talking about sports. He noticed that they received little physical exercise—it was years before the Special Olympics. He approached the principal and suggested a modest exercise program. She readily gave permission.

He took the boys to a small yard adjoining the school. (He still didn't know what to do with the girls.) He began with a few simple exercises, little more than standing on their toes. What suprised him was that these young men—ages fourteen to twenty-five—actually enjoyed the workout. There were smiles and laughter.

"I had them walk on their heels, then on their hands and feet," he said. He told them to pretend that they were bears looking for honey. Some fell down, but they seemed to enjoy the falls as much as the exercise. "They were really into it."

More exercises followed. They learned to walk on the sides of their feet—a simple, fun exercise. "They were doing the oldest thing in the world," Bob recalled. "They were having fun."

The first few days of exercises taught the future co-founder of the Lambs Farm two things: First, that the retarded are relatively resourceless. They can be passive, inert, and unimaginative people. There is very little they can do on their own. They need other people to make them be what they can be. Second, the retarded can learn. They can recognize what is expected of them, repeat it back, and enjoy it when they do it.

Bob began to mix the exercises and to increase the speed at which he changed commands. Most of his students followed him. They were retaining and applying knowledge.

As the exercises grew more complex, not every student was able to keep up. Bob was learning something about ability levels. The students were learning to be themselves, to have fun, to experience their own bodies.

Winter comes early and stays late in the Midwest. Soon the students had to go inside, and the exercise space was limited. Bob needed to think of other things for them to do.

Not long after, the parents were able to hire a full-time teacher for the older students. She was Jean Adams, who had befriended Bob during a difficult period in his life. With her husband, she introduced him to her church. Later she would introduce him to Corinne Owen.

Like Bob, Jean had no special training in the education of

the retarded but was willing to be innovative. The parents, however, still insisted on an academic approach to learning, and Jean was required to stick to the standard curriculum. Bob did some indoor exercises with the students, but for the rest, he was stymied.

Bonaparte School had a kitchen, however. Gradually, Bob came to the conclusion that these young students could learn to cook. "Cooking is one of the most basic skills," he said. "These young people might never have to cook, but at least they could help their mothers. At least they could learn to cook a hot dog."

Most of the students loved it. They learned simple, basic cooking: hot dogs, Jell-O, bean casseroles. The tasks were broken down—a method that Corinne Owen would later perfect. One student opened the can of beans; a second would cut up the wieners; a third would sprinkle the brown sugar over the mix, which was being stirred by a fourth. Each had a role in the project. Each received praise for his or her accomplishment.

In the months ahead, Bob discovered that the retarded can learn practical skills and carry them out. He came to realize that the retarded have varying abilities and need to be trained accordingly. These realizations came with their own burdens. Parents of the more severely retarded were upset when their children were not taught to cook. Some children were so learning disabled that they could barely communicate. But Bob felt strongly that the curriculum could not cater to the lowest common denominator and that the brighter students could not be held back in order to meet the needs of the less able. Understandably, board members of the school were trying to be evenhanded about all students.

In the spring of 1958, Bob was hired as a full-time teacher. Bonaparte parents were not wealthy. His salary was minuscule. He still worked nights on the railroad, but the school was the focus of his life.

When Jean Adams reluctantly resigned to have her baby, she recommended that Corinne Owen take her place.

Corinne knew nothing about the retarded; later she vaguely recalled having one piano student who she thought might "be a little slow." She had teaching skills, however, skills gained during years of a largely tutorial approach to learning. They were honed even more through several years of selling a quality reading program. She could persuade through her innate sincerity and her clarity of expression. She was looking for a new challenge.

Bob was not at the school the day Corinne came for her interview visit. During the summer before her arrival, she grew increasingly anxious about the program and her teaching partner. Finally, Jean Adams arranged a meeting at Jean and Corinne's church, which Bob had recently joined.

Corinne was not impressed. Her world was carefully organized. She arranged lesson plans in three colors on poster-size cardboard. She sensed that Bob operated on instinct. He stood around, folding his arms and hitching up his pants, answering only, "It'll be all right."

For his part, Bob thought Corinne rigid, brittle, reserved, methodical. "One of those Baptists," he concluded. "You're too German," he would say to her later when she tried to put some methodological substance into one of his visionary plans.

While they exaggerated each other's shortcomings, neither was entirely wrong. Bob often operates on the fumes of his imagination; Corinne is practical. The combination would later prove a boon to the pair. Corinne would put structure into Bob's ideas. She would break his concepts down into parts that could be translated into learning units for the students. Bob provided the music; Corinne supplied the notes. Bob has a short fuse; Corinne has endless patience. According to Bob, she can "endure ugliness and temper tantrums. She could turn a troubled, fearful child into a calm, affectionate one."

Although her voice is mild—one often must strain to hear her—Corinne can stand her ground. She can cling to an idea like a limpet; she can argue with Bob—and often has. However, in things that mattered, they were joined at the hip.

The disparate emotional chemistry of the two made for an ideal combination.

Within five minutes after Corinne first arrived at Bonaparte, a young boy named Bruce threw his arms around her neck and told her he loved her. Corinne had few emotional adjustment problems at Bonaparte. She was hooked from the start. She spent the first day observing, then got down to work.

It is said that students affect teachers about as much as teachers affect students. In this case, the maxim applies completely. Corinne Owen and Bob Terese are now so assimilated into the community of the retarded that they prefer the companionship of the Lambs to that of so-called normal people. They do not reject the able-minded. It is simply that they have found a kind of emotional Eden in the unfiltered, unvarnished world of their special people.

She began to take a few students at a time to a separate room and to attempt to evaluate their separate skills. With no firm curriculum at Bonaparte, both teachers often arrived each morning with new and disparate ideas. "We would often just stare each other down until one of us got our way," Corinne recalled.

It soon became clear to each of them, however, that their ideas coincided. Corinne's reading workbooks contained sentences with cards that the retarded could be taught to complete and with essential words such as *men* and *ladies*, *fire* and *danger*. She taught them about the weather and the seasons, and about the major holidays of the year. Then they celebrated the holidays.

Before long Corinne came to recognize that her students were not possessed of equal ability. She broke them into three groups—those with limited ability, with whom she discussed the individual words they needed to recognize; those who could do some basic reading; and those who could read and also investigate why things worked. She didn't realize it then, but Corinne was forming the basis of an approach to educating the retarded that would be the core of the learning processes at the Lambs Farm until this day.

The new approach met with some resistance. Parents of the less able students felt that their children were being cheated. Frequently, when the new approach was broached to the school's board, the teachers were asked, "Is this for *all* the students?" The parents were being sincerely solicitous. All were contributing to the school; all should share equally in its benefits. But, in their effort to be all things to all students, they overlooked the fact that equality consists of treating unequal things unequally.

Corinne agreed with Bob's initial observation that much of the learning had little real link with the students' lived experience. She began to teach them about the days of the week and the months of the year. Those who could learn were taught how to tell time. When the weather was good, she took them to the adjoining Morton Arboretum and introduced them to nature. They were fascinated by nature. They asked questions. They learned—and Bob and Corinne learned something about how they learned.

Jean Adams had left the school but continued to volunteer her efforts as much as time would allow. Her husband, Ed, an art professor at Wheaton College, offered to teach the students silk-screening. By this time, Corinne had joined Bob in the downstairs classroom and was eager to be part of the silk-screening process.

They bought the silk-screening material with funds left over from the cooking effort. Mrs. Kopecky cut the stencils for the students; Bob and Corinne attempted to print them.

The first results were messy. Some prints refused to dry. It took Ed Adams to point out to the teachers that they were using ink intended for cloth, not paper. "The directions were right on the can," Bob recalled. "But who looks there?" The teachers were learning.

The parents liked the results. They bought the Christmas cards their children produced. The project made a modest profit, which was spent on a Christmas party. Now the parents were learning something.

The cooking and the card making led to playing store. The students were already accompanying Bob or Corinne to the supermarket but were unable to recognize products. A play store was set up at the school, and in time the students learned to identify products. Most couldn't read, but they could identify colors, shapes, and sizes. It took time, but the concept worked. Corinne stocked the shelves, then patiently asked each student to bring her an item. It was a method Corinne and her students would use later at their State Street pet store. They never dreamed that these projects would become the ingredients of the many business enterprises at the Farm.

Bob Terese sees his professional growth at Bonaparte as conceptually akin to the experience of the visitors, especially church and senior citizen groups, at the Lambs Farm today. "At first, they're reluctant. But they come to avail themselves of our dining room; they visit the stores. Our Lambs meet them and show them around. They leave excited about what they've seen. The next time they meet a retarded person, the process of getting through their handicaps will be more remote. Soon all they will see is a person. Furthermore, our population is made up of the moderately retarded. Once people come to know them, they will be better able to understand the severely and profoundly retarded. It's a process."

Corinne and Bob wanted to learn more. What they had more or less stumbled upon was working, but they weren't certain. They arranged a visit to a nearby private school for the retarded in the shared hope of learning something more.

What they found was terribly disturbing. Young, diapered children were housed in wooden pens. Many were hyperactive and screaming, kicking the sides of their pens. A flickering TV was on the wall—the only diversion for them. "Just look at what I've got to take care of!" the matronly teacher said. Bob later recalled that lab rats at universities get better care. In another class, children were being taught to "read"—a process that was nothing more than continual drill until they had memorized a meaningless passage. The lack of interest was as palpable as the pervasive smell of urine.

Corinne asked, "Is there anything they like?" The director replied that they seemed to like the music they heard when students from a nearby church-related college conducted Sunday school. When asked why there was no music during the week, the teacher responded, "They get enough of that on Sunday."

Corinne and Bob were barely back to the car when Corinne announced, "We're going to sing. We're going to do a minstrel show. We're going to show the parents what their children can do. We're going to sing all week!"

It was a three-hanky show. First there were Christmas carols. Then the minstrels sang and danced. Tears streamed down the parents' cheeks when they saw their children perform.

By this time, Corinne and Bob were staying later with the students. The short day eventually was lengthened until 2:00 P.M. Still, the students didn't want to go home. Neither did Corinne or Bob, who were experiencing the greatest job satisfaction in their lives.

One day, Corinne wondered aloud about the future of the students. What would they do when their schooling ended? The question so haunted Bob that he went home that evening and attempted to write a prospectus for the students' lives. It was a rough plan for a store—one that involved the retarded and that would support a home for the retarded. The store was nearly four years away. But that night a dream was born, one that wouldn't go away.

◆ Lambs Tales ◆
Jim

After three decades of working with retarded adults, Bob Terese observed, "Perhaps the greatest obstacle to the retarded child's adjustment to the normal world is fear. A retarded child fears the world which has held up normality as the only possible standard. The child is then ridiculed if he or she fails to meet it. And more than fear of the world, it is this fear of failure—repeated failures to learn, to act, to be, to get along, even to enjoy—that haunts the retarded child."

Jim was just such a case. He was eighteeen when he came to the Lambs Pet Store. He had a dreary background of academic failures. He hadn't been able to get along, even in the special schools. Almost an adult, his only satisfaction came in playing on the floor with model cars. He was good at that. A lifetime of failure had taught him to settle for next to nothing.

When he came to the Lambs Pet Store on State Street, he had no work habits, no imagination, no initiative. He hid behind a severe case of hypochondria. He couldn't work because he had a headache or backache, a toothache or earache. The imaginary aches masked a real, deeper ache. Jim was terrified that he would not be able to do what he was asked to do. If he fumbled a task Bob or Corinne asked him to do, he could always point to an illness.

"Jim was correct," Bob recalled. "He was sick—sick with fear and sick with self-concern, sick that he would fail again."

Corinne finally persuaded him to take charge of the animals who had to visit the veterinarian. Taking care of the sick puppies brought him out of himself. Gradually, he forgot his own imagined ailments as he absorbed the real ones of the lovable animals. More important, he grew more sure of himself.

When a puppy got sick, Jim was told to place it in a basket next to the cash register, where it could be warm and where Corinne or Bob could also keep an eye on it. For Jim, then, the place next to the register was for puppies when they were sick.

It must be remembered that, generally speaking, retarded persons are single-minded, tenacious about what they have learned, and resistant to any alteration of that information. Jim would later go on to take a full-time job in a bakery stockroom—in fact, he would be placed in charge of it—but at this point in his life, he was extremely brittle and self-absorbed.

One day, not long before Christmas, the pet store received a shipment of poodle puppies. It was the custom to bathe all new puppies, and this was done. With the rush of Christmas traffic, however, the half-dozen poodles were left in a basket near the register to dry.

When the phone next to the register rang, a cooler, more confident Jim answered. "Oh, yes," Corinne heard him say. "We have four or five poodles. But every single one of them is sick!"

◆ Chapter 3 ◆

Hull House

The Bonaparte School did not have summer classes, so Bob Terese needed a summer job. It came through Marilyn Miller, a fellow member of the Wheaton Baptist Church. She was a teacher at Retarded Children's Aid (RCA) in the vast Hull House complex on Chicago's near West Side.

Another teacher at RCA wanted the summer off, and the organization needed a gym instructor and teacher. Bob could use the money. He was still working for the Milwaukee Road but had cut his hours somewhat in order to devote more time to his teaching. The railroad job remained boring; Bob wanted to quit but had accumulated some seniority and retirement benefits. He would have to wait.

In that summer of 1959, Corinne received an opportunity to attend classes at the University of Illinois at Champaign-Urbana. A superintendent of special education in the Du Page County school system had recommended her, and the local Lions Club had provided the scholarship. Bonaparte School had no teachers who had completed course work in special education. Corinne was glad of the opportunity.

It was a long summer. Corinne commuted weekly to her classes, living in a modest room on the campus. While tuition was provided, she had limited personal funds, barely enough to eat. She learned a lot and lost a lot of weight.

While at the University of Illinois, she raised the question of whether the retarded could work with other people in the operation of a store. She received a very cool reception. On balance, the experts simply didn't listen. They had measured the limits of the retarded; they would set those boundaries.

For Corinne and Bob, ideological conflict with professionals was to be a part of their lives for the next two decades. In the years ahead, they would be invited to serve on state and federal committees—including the President's Committee on the Handicapped. They would speak at nine universities and before innumerable parent groups. Groups working with the retarded came from as far away as Japan and Israel to study the Lambs Farm approach. Yet, when the nationally televised documentary program "20/20" did a feature on the Farm, one academician wrote to the program's producers and attempted to stop the broadcast. "I've never gotten such a letter prior to a broadcast," the ABC producer said.

Perhaps it was Corinne's and Bob's failure to follow the professional pathways. Bob had always marched to the beat of a different drummer; Corinne was so trusting that she missed signs of opposition. Whatever the case, they were a threat to the existing system. The professional community consisted of university professors, agency leaders, and owners of elite private care homes. A music teacher and a physical education major—neither with college degrees in their field or with course work on the learning disabled—were not going to dictate to the system. It would be years before the Lambs Farm concept received full-blown recognition.

At summer's end, the teacher whom Bob had replaced announced that he did not want to return to Hull House. Bob was offered his position. It was a full-time job, and the salary was better than at the Bonaparte School; he could reduce his hours on the railroad.

It was hard to leave Bonaparte, harder still to leave Corinne. But the RCA facility represented a larger playing field on which he could learn a great deal more. He took the job.

Hull House was founded by Jane Addams and Ellen Gates Starr in 1889. What came to be known as "the cathedral of compassion" began in an old mansion at what is now the intersection of Halsted and Polk streets. Over the years, the "Great Experiment," as it was called, expanded to a complex of thirteen buildings that filled an entire city block. It became one of America's best-known settlement houses.

Hull House was more than just a reform outpost in the slums. It became part of a cultural renaissance in Chicago— all this despite being located in a neighborhood that journalist Lincoln Steffens described as "first in violence, deepest in dirt, loud, lawless, unlovely, ill-smelling, criminally wide open, commercially brazen, socially thoughtless and raw."

"Hull House residents came from many walks of life," wrote Wallace Kirkland, a former social worker, in an unpublished memoir sometime in the late 1920s. "They were people who worked in other parts of the city, who wanted to live and share their talents with the less fortunate people of the neighborhood. They were doctors, lawyers, college professors, schoolteachers, social workers, students, musicians, actors, writers, poets, artists, politicians." It was good soil in which Retarded Children's Aid could grow.

By the 1920s, it was estimated that more than 9,000 people went to the settlement house weekly to take advantage of its activities. The complex flourished for many years. In 1962, however, eleven of the buildings were demolished to make room for what is now the University of Illinois at Chicago. Only the original Charles J. Hull mansion and the residents' dining hall remain. They are landmarks and museums preserved to honor Jane Addams, who died in 1935 at age seventy-four.

In 1959, Retarded Children's Aid was part of the Hull House complex. It attempted to meet the needs of several hundred retarded persons representing a wide variety of ability levels.

Bob Terese thinks like an artist. He gets impressions. His first impression of the RCA facility was ashtrays. Poorly made, garish, misshapen, they virtually littered the facility. There were four or five on every table; the storage cabinets were filled with them. When he asked Marilyn Miller about them, she was embarrassed. "The young people have a ceramics class here once a week," she explained. "So far, all they have learned to make is ashtrays. I guess the parents have enough of them. We keep the leftovers here."

All Bob Terese could think of was the sanded and lacquered plates back at the Bonaparte School.

Again, he didn't know the answer. The parents and teachers at RCA were working with a restricted budget and in overcrowded conditions. Making ashtrays represented progress and an effort to be creative. Parents of the RCA community had witnessed situations in which the mentally disabled had simply sat on benches for endless hours, rocking back and forth in some subconscious effort to burn energy. Ashtrays represented activity and a measure of learning.

The ashtrays were not the only repetitive task Bob would witness. Sometimes, in the sheltered workshops, after the contracted work was completed, the supervisors would dump boxloads of nuts and bolts on the worktables. The retarded would attach the nuts to the bolts, only to separate them later for reassembly at another time. It was neither cruel nor unusual treatment—just a desperate effort to keep large numbers of young people occupied.

There had to be a better way. Bob continued to observe and to dream.

Retarded Children's Aid had divided its membership into three programs. The low retarded were housed in the Jane Club, where a talented teacher named Jackson played and sang with them for most of the day. It worked well, and it was pretty much all their abilities permitted.

The middle-level retarded worked in a sheltered workshop in another building. In the 1950s, sheltered workshops were a genuine innovation, and the Retarded Children's Aid Society was the pioneer in the Chicago area. Earlier, while Bob was still at Bonaparte School, he had visited the workshop and introduced the concept at Bonaparte. The director of the workshop at RCA had designed a wooden frame that held a dozen nuts and bolts. Since most of the students could not count, they only needed to fill up the frame and then transfer the nuts and bolts into a bag. The packaging was repetitive and unimaginative work, but it was preferable to sanding and lacquering.

At RCA, the workshop concept was enjoying real success. It often had an overflow of work. The low-level factory work appealed to the retarded. They have a high tolerance for repetitive work. Once trained to do a task, they rarely make mistakes. They are energetic workers, and they enjoy the sense of accomplishment.

In the years ahead, Bob and Corinne would have an uneven relationship with the sheltered-workshop concept. The philosophy of the Lambs Farm was intended to break away from such methods, to press the retarded toward further progress. However, decades of experience convinced them that not everyone was geared to more imaginative tasks. Bob and Corinne have come to accept the practice of sheltered workshops as necessary and worthwhile.

At the Lambs Farm, the sheltered-workshop program involves at least 25 percent of the residents. The facility, located just a few miles from the Farm, contracts with a wide variety of companies for short- and long-term tasks. The participants can move from one task to another; they are trained and evaluated; they are paid for their efforts and even enjoy the privilege of paying taxes. "We started the Lambs Farm to get away from all this," Bob recalled. "But it's necessary, and it's good. Corinne and I have come to terms with it."

The third ability group at RCA consisted of the "mavericks" from the sheltered workshop. These were the higher-functioning young adults who found the sheltered workshop concept boring and frustrating. They were gathered on the second floor of the Jane Club, a building that had originally contained apartments for working girls. In fact, a number of retired teachers were still living in the building's upper two floors. It was a pleasant, homelike atmosphere. Bob and Marilyn Miller worked well together.

In the months that followed, Bob settled in. Without Corinne, with whom he could always share ideas, he found that his ability to generate new ideas slowed somewhat, but he was not uncomfortable. Exposed all day to the mildly and moderately retarded, he gradually got to understand them better.

During the winter of 1959–1960, Marilyn Miller became ill and had to resign. She encouraged Corinne to apply. Corinne was hesitant at first. RCA was an established facility with a national reputation. The parents of the Bonaparte children didn't want to see her leave but were pleased for her. They gave her a glowing letter of recommendation. By late winter, Corinne and Bob were working together again.

"The first thing we'll do is paint the place," Corinne said. "I can't imagine anyone doing anything here." The place *was* pretty dreary, Bob recalled later.

The students would work with them, they decided. The director scoffed. He gave his permission but added, "These kids? They can't paint. They haven't got the ability. Go ahead, but it's your funeral."

Bob Terese recalled years later that the painting incident capsulized the differing points of view of the professional bureaucrat and Corinne and Bob. The bureaucrat had a custodial attitude: keep them busy, keep them working, keep them quiet, keep them under control. Bob and Corinne wanted to challenge them, to get them to do work they enjoyed, to keep them happy. They weren't concerned about failure, only about challenging their charges.

The director was consumed with making things "look good." Appearances were terribly important to him. In fairness, such appearances often determined funding. In one telling incident, the young people were asked to provide a cake for the 100th birthday of the City of Chicago. It was to be presented to then-mayor Richard J. Daley in his City Hall office. The director ordered Corinne to make the cake. "Make it look good. Make it a tier cake. That will be really special," he told her.

The irony was that Corinne had no experience in making a tiered cake. In fact, following her wedding years before, it was her husband, Trevor, who cooked the first home meal.

Corinne has never been a cook, much less a baker. The young people at RCA could bake a respectable sheet cake with Corinne's help. But this one had to "look good." So Corinne did as she was told. The tiered cake was presented to the mayor, but by the time it got to the mayor's office, it leaned like the Tower of Pisa. It didn't even "look good."

Painting the rooms was a slow process. The students loved it, however. These were *their* rooms. This was *their* paint job. A young Japanese man, the oldest of the group, fell off the ladder twice. His black hair was covered with yellow paint, but he wouldn't stop. He could put paint on walls. He could *do* something. It wasn't just busywork. It wasn't simply putting puzzles together—dog-eared puzzles they had completed perhaps a hundred times before. It was not just mumbling into a tape recorder, a meaningless process called "speech therapy." They could do this task and talk about it.

Corinne and Bob recalled the hikes they took with the Bonaparte students at the wondrous Morton Arboretum. They remembered the acorns they collected in the fall and how they shellacked them and strung them with yarn. Hull House wasn't near such beautiful settings, but there was a lot to see in Chicago.

The retarded are not invalids. An estimated 50 percent suffer from some physical disbility, but, with proper therapy, they can function without difficulty. Attitudinal problems by their caregivers, however, kept them isolated and inactive, as if they were invalids.

Loving parents often grow weary of the struggle to train their handicapped children. As a consequence, they find it easier simply to do the task for their retarded children, thus leaving them even more dependent. The retarded themselves can be very resistant to caregivers, largely because of a deep-seated fear of failure. It sets up a kind of emotional downward spiral.

The healthy retarded have boundless energy, however. Once trained to a task, they can do it with great efficiency. The stereotype of the slow-moving, pear-shaped Down's syndrome person, for example, is now on the wane. With proper diet and exercise, such people can trim down to normal weight levels. At the Lambs Farm, a vigorous exercise program now helps many residents to keep fit. Ironically, because the retarded have a higher tolerance for repetitive activities, they can remain on the exercise bikes for long periods, thus toning muscles and reducing weight more efficiently than the able-bodied. At the Lambs Farm, the exercise room is among the most used facilities in the complex.

"We wanted to give them a chance to see the world, to show them that they were as much a part of the world as their normal brothers and sisters," Bob recalled.

The practice of overhelping or overprotecting the mentally handicapped has been likened to what the physically handicapped have had to endure. Unable to move about in a normal fashion, they have often been denied access to related opportunities. Thus, a woman born without arms or legs was given loving care by her mother, who bathed her, dressed her, and wheeled her around. At sixteen, she was still unable to dress herself. She realized, however, that her caring mother had never given her the opportunity even to select the color of the dresses she would wear. Similarly, parents of retarded children, thinking that there was little they could learn at the zoo, would leave them in the care of a sitter and take their able-minded children to see the animals. Today, thanks to a more enlightened viewpoint, it is difficult to visit a zoo without encountering groups of retarded people enjoying the same sights and sounds as their fellow citizens.

At Retarded Children's Aid, the first field trips were organized around food, related to cooking classes inspired by those initiated at the Bonaparte School. Since the young people at RCA had higher ability levels, they were preparing more sophisticated dishes. The area around the Hull House complex was a rich mix of ethnic stores and restaurants, especially Greek, Mexican, and Italian. The group visited the stores and gained experience purchasing the ingredients for the meals they would later prepare. At Jane House, they would watch a movie on Italy, then they would go to an

Italian grocery store and purchase food they had seen in the movie. They would bring it back to the center and prepare their version of an Italian meal.

More important, they met people; they learned to talk to them. The young mentally retarded overcame the small fears that haunt those who have experienced rejection. They also helped the nonretarded to put aside their irrational fears.

From the local stores, the group ventured to the colorful, noisy South Water Market area of the city, a wonderfully tacky rosary of stores and warehouses where the city's fruits, vegetables, flowers, and some meats are sold. The freewheeling, hardworking, eccentric store owners—used to bargaining endlessly with the public—greeted the RCA group with tolerance and kindness.

The South Water Market is not a bank lobby or the mall of an elite shopping center. It is a big, burly place with a heart of gold. The food is displayed in crates, sometimes still on the back of the trucks on which it arrived. Buyers shout at sellers as they tap the crates with their pencils, indicating what they want.

For the RCA members, it was a wondrous world, one in which buyers paid cash for a truckload of watermelons, for example, but wouldn't dream of paying for a single melon any more than a Chicago cop on the beat would pay for a pushcart apple. The market men would hand the group a ripe watermelon. Street etiquette required that it be consumed on the spot. The twenty or more tourists would sit on the garbage-stained curb, slice the melon, savor its juices, and throw the rinds in the gutter. "I never get to do this at home," one shouted gleefully.

Bob recalled, "Back at Bonaparte School, I had to teach them to walk on the sides of their feet. They had lost their ability to create their own fun. At the Water Street Market, they got an endless supply of new experiences. They were absorbing new information. Now they could ask where these fruits came from. They learned how things grew, where they grew, how they got to market. The street was a symphony of sounds and smells. There were few prohibitions. They could see, smell, taste—and ask. They weren't just putting the same puzzle together for the fiftieth time. Now they were not resourceless. It greatly improved their verbal skills. When they got home, they had something to tell their parents.

"We used to bring them flowers and leaves from the country," Corinne said. "We would then teach them how to dry the flowers and how to decorate baskets with them. When the painting was complete, they did window boxes with flowers and cared for them. They learned so much! And I enjoyed myself so much that I didn't think I should be paid for working at Hull House."

There was another significant benefit. The parents of the higher-functioning RCA students wanted their children to someday leave the sheltered-workshop environment and find employment at an outside job. Frequently, however, because of their sheltered environment, they never got the opportunity to develop the social skills necessary to human interaction. They could do the assigned job but were often too shy, embarrassed, or frightened—or belligerent, dominating, and hostile—to get along with others. ("Bennie," the retarded character in the popular TV series "L.A. Law," depicts this entire range of emotions so credibly that he has been honored by groups who work with the mentally disabled.) The field trips brought them to the public and gave them an opportunity to interact with expansive, tolerant people. They gained poise and confidence.

At Jane House, Corinne was holding fashion shows for the women. The models wore their own clothes, topped with handmade bands of flowers around their heads. The style shows gave them an opportunity to walk in front of people, to overcome fear, to develop poise. Sometimes the young men also took part, and both groups performed together in occasional minstrel shows.

When Bob and Corinne attempted to introduce silk-screening at Hull House, they ran into just one of many philosophical and practical conflicts they would have with the director. The director was not always open to new ideas. Like many bureaucrats, he saw his job as consisting of carrying out a preapproved program. The retarded were consigned to RCA for custodial care. Keep them happy, content, safe, but don't try to upgrade them. It wouldn't work. The retarded were fixed stars. There were budget considerations. Besides, a project must be proven successful before it could be undertaken.

"How much will it cost?" he asked. "How many cards can they do in a day? How are we going to sell them? Wholesale or retail?" The notion of trying something for its own sake was beyond his comprehension. "We only wanted to run it up the flagpole," Bob said. But, under this man's hesitant leadership, there would be no flagpoles.

It was a difficult period for RCA. At that time, there were many philosophical differences involving approaches to the treatment of the retarded. At RCA, the director insisted on a common denominator of uniform custodial care as the primary objective. The leader of the sheltered-workshop program was convinced that there was a task for all retarded within the workshop framework. There was some evidence that the lower-functioning students could do more than sing, dance, and finger-paint. It was equally obvious that some of the middle-range students benefited so much from the sheltered-workshop concept that they were eventually able to move into the upper-level program. At this time, however, each program had its advocates, and tension ran high.

Unwittingly, parents contributed to the conflict. It was the parents who provided most of the money to support RCA. The parents, understandably, were interested in supporting the level of the program that best benefited their child. Bob recalled: "Little thought was given to either the children or the program in general; the polarization was dictated by private interest alone."

In the years that followed, Retarded Children's Aid became part of the Chicago Association for the Mentally Retarded. It has evolved into an excellent program, meeting the needs of hundreds of retarded adults. The political and ideological tensions that Bob and Corinne encountered at RCA in 1959, however, served as a catalyst to their thinking about the development of the Lambs Farm.

Their experience at RCA convinced them that their talents could best be used in working with the moderate- to high-functioning disabled in an entirely different environment—and the sooner the better.

Corinne and Bob were able to stay above the fray. Their rooms on the second floor of Jane House became a kind of haven for many of the students who were bored by the sheltered-workshop program. The workshop staffers were glad to see that the higher-functioning were moving to Bob and Corinne's classes. These brighter students upset the rhythms of the shelter program by working faster than the other students or, worse, by acting out. At Jane House, they could learn to cook, go on tours, silk-screen cards. They were not simply robots on a production line, putting nuts and bolts in bags.

Bob and Corinne recognized that these young adults could be pressed to do more. They recognized that their own projects had the potential of becoming just as boring. They continued to discuss the unheard-of notion of developing a program for them that would provide for a wide range of experiences based on participants' capabilities. Further, the program could provide income for its participants, so that they would not be totally reliant upon their parents. Bob and Corinne began to think of a community—a place to live—not simply a program for a working day, but one that would embrace their entire lives.

Initially, they thought about food. Their students could prepare salads, casseroles, and the like. A catering service sounded good. They approached the Illinois Council on Mental Retardation and received a measure of encouragement. The director suggested a pancake house as preferable to catering. She had a point. In such a setting, the retarded could work directly with the public.

They visited a thriving pancake restaurant in Evanston, Illinois. After careful review, it was obvious to Corinne and Bob that these RCA members were not quite ready for an operation that proved more complex than they had imagined. Further, they concluded that the public was not yet ready to deal with retarded adults. There were simply too many prejudices. Gradually, too, they came to the conclusion that the catering business wouldn't work—at least not at that time.

But they had to do something. The politics at RCA had gotten so tense that the parents had been forced to replace both the director and the supervisor of the sheltered workshop. Initially, the new administrators were willing to listen to ideas, but as they tackled the practical problems of administering a complex organization that continued to grow rapidly, they had little time for radical ideas.

Sometime during his college years, Bob Terese had worked for a summer at Van Oak's Pet Store on Chicago's North Avenue. The experience did not turn him into a pet lover, but while searching for something for his charges, he considered the qualities the retarded possessed in abundance, especially their ability to give and receive love.

He couldn't wait until the next day. He called Corinne that evening and announced, "I've got it. A pet store!" She agreed on the spot.

When he picked Corinne up the next morning, he had already thought of a name for the store. "We'll call it 'The Lambs,' " he said. Corinne knew well the passage from St. John's gospel where Christ tells his disciples, "Feed my lambs." She recalled that many of the students had pets at home, and she remembered her experiences with her students, teaching them to play store. It seemed like a perfect fit.

They began talking to some of the parents of their charges and to parents of the Bonaparte students. The parents liked the idea, especially if the business had the potential of supporting a home. Virtually all parents of retarded children worry about the time they will not be able to provide a home for their retarded son or daughter. This might be a partial answer.

Among the most interested were the parents of Steve Buell, a former student from the Bonaparte School, whom

Bob still worked with at a Sunday exercise class he led in Elmhurst. Mrs. Buell told him of a Delilah White at the Levenson Foundation. "Delilah had a similiar idea several years ago," the Buells told Bob and Corinne. "You really ought to talk to her."

Delilah T. White came to Chicago in 1945. A graduate of the University of Cincinnati, where she earned her master's degree in psychology, she was a divorcée with two children. Her former husband had been generous in the divorce settlement, but she found that the homemaker's life in the suburbs did not offer a challenge. She obtained a job in the Evanston public schools, where she had an opportunity to develop a full range of ideas, many of which would later have application to the education of the mentally disabled. After a brief experiment living in her native Texas, where she gained experience evaluating children with cerebral palsy—some 14 percent of whom are retarded—she returned to Illinois for a position in the Rockford area. The city proved a bit too rural for Delilah, however, and when the state opened an office in the Chicago suburb of Glencoe, she happily returned to nearby Evanston to make her home.

After several years' work with blind, deaf, and retarded children, she came to the conclusion that the physically and/or mentally handicapped could not be properly evaluated or treated without a complete examination that would evaluate all of the facts that constitute a profile. At that time, retarded people were often evaluated in isolation. Their physical handicaps often masked their mental handicaps and vice versa. Further, treatment was often compartmentalized so that caretakers had to choose whether to seek physical or mental help. That approach led to confusing and frustrating conflicts and did not address the needs of the whole child.

Delilah attended a conference in Fort Wayne, Indiana, where she heard and was later introduced to Abraham Levenson, M.D., a man who shared her vision. "He needed a ride back to Chicago," she recalled years later. "We talked all the way. We just clicked."

Shortly after, he confided to her that he was thinking of opening a clinic. (It would later be called the Levenson Center for the Mentally Handicapped.) He needed a psychologist and offered the position to Delilah.

Four years after White joined the clinic, Abraham Levenson died. She was asked to become the clinic's director, a position she held for twenty-three years.

With a group of interested parents, Corinne and Bob visited Delilah White at her Chestnut Street apartment. She told them of her experience with Little City, another independent facility for the retarded, located in Palatine, Illinois. Some years before, with the aid of interested and energetic parents, White had designed the operational philosophy of Little City and become its professional director. It was a concept not unlike that of Corinne and Bob's: a community of retarded people who would meet most of their own needs. Further, she had hoped to do significant research with her charges. However, differing viewpoints on goals and job descriptions, budget problems, and some understandable internal politics caused conflicts, and after a few years, Delilah White resigned. (Little City continues to this day, an outstanding facility for the mentally handicapped.)

After a rest in Sarasota, Florida, Delilah returned to private practice and part-time work at the Levenson Clinic. When the idea of the Lambs Pet Store came along, she was ready to become involved. She believed that the dream she had for Little City could find a home at the store.

Delilah White contributed her services from the start. She did the professional evaluations of the initial members of the Lambs' community. Just as important, she made numerous contacts among her well-placed friends to get advice and financial support. She brought professional credentials to the first efforts of the community and defended Bob and Corinne from some of the criticism being leveled at them. "You know, formal education blunts our instincts at times," she said in 1989. "Bob and Corinne are naturally competent. They have their love to give and a great many spiritual insights."

By the early 1960s, Delilah White had achieved an international reputation. She was delivering research papers in places such as Vienna and Copenhagen. She was telling her listeners that people were selling Down's syndrome children short. She was urging parents, "Don't be good to your children. Make them do it!" She maintained that retarded adults can meet many of their own needs and that they need to be lovingly prodded. Of course, it takes time and often infinite patience, but they can learn. To a rich man with a retarded son, she said, "He's only upsetting your pride!" She was quoting then-president John F. Kennedy, who was then telling America, "Every retarded child can be helped."

White recognized the many faces and the many treatment techniques within the extended family of the mentally handicapped. "You can't put a smooth blanket over retardation," she said. "My heart goes out to the parents. They often have to sacrifice their other children." She rebelled against false sympathy or any attempt to keep retarded children confined to home or to an institution. She urged stimulation. In short, she was echoing the very sentiments of the founders of the Lambs Farm. At a time when individuals and organizations in the profession were refusing to talk to Bob or Corinne, her seal of approval was invaluable.

"I don't care if you have to start your pet store in a basement," she told them, "you go ahead and do it. Don't let anyone stand in your way. This kind of program—giving the retarded meaningful employment in a sheltered situation—is absolutely essential.

"Keep it simple," she added. "Keep it directed only to young people. Your profits are only for them."

Keeping it simple wasn't all that simple. There were twelve parents on the initial advisory board. Each had strong ideas born of long and sometimes painful experience. All the interests had to be balanced without a loss of focus. For Corinne and Bob, it was a lesson in leadership.

Initially, the founders intended to establish the Lambs Pet Store through the RCA. They had hoped to establish a partnership between the RCA and the store. They failed to understand the chemistry of bureaucracies.

When they approached the director, he listened with growing impatience. He leaned back in his chair and responded, "Well, I'll tell you. There's a bulletin board here behind my desk. You can stick your idea up there with the hundred other ideas I get." He saw himself as a harried administrator. New ideas were thorns in his side. He had not had experience with the retarded; he simply arranged paper. One idea was no different from any other. All were threatening.

Nonetheless, Corinne and Bob continued to make contacts. More parents became interested. Corinne and Bob freely admit to being naive. RCA had a waiting list; they assumed that any effort to ease the burden and to accommodate more participants would be welcomed.

They returned to the director and asked to hold a discussion meeting with the board members of RCA. They were bemused when the director never even informed his board.

At a subsequent meeting in Delilah White's apartment, they decided to prepare a little brochure to be passed out at the annual Christmas Style Show. The brochure was nothing more than a six-paragraph mimeographed letter, but it might as well have been a revolutionary tract. It simply invited the parents to consider the establishment of a pet store to be staffed by retarded adults. Bob and Corinne were only vaguely aware that the idea had never been formally introduced to the parents. Thus, the one-page invitation was seen as a radical departure from the status quo.

The RCA board had just recovered from one transition period. Now two employees were attempting to start a new venture without the board's knowledge or consent. The board members saw the action as subversive and a threat to their authority. They were furious.

Just two weeks before Christmas 1960, speaking for the board, the director offered Bob and Corinne a chance to enroll at the University of Chicago to take professional courses. RCA would pay all expenses. He also promised to make Corinne the head of the social department and Bob the head of the physical education department. All they had to do was to promise to give up any more talk or action about the proposed Lambs Pet Store.

They answered, "No."

He fired them on the spot.

♦ Lambs Tales ♦
"I'm One of Them"

It was bound to happen someday. It did about a year after the Lambs Pet Store on State Street was opened.

She exuded money. Some would call it class, but clearly the only class she had was in her clothes—a mink hat over a black-and-white tweed suit. This was a Gold Coast matron— someone who didn't need a reservation at a top restaurant. Her money gave her confidence and power. It didn't give her sensitivity.

She began a rapid, almost impatient tour of the store. It was hard to determine what she wanted.

Finally, in a tone of voice that exuded condescension, she said, "I hear you have retarded boys and girls here. Where are they?"

The question was delivered as if she expected to find the mentally handicapped in cages. Bob Terese has a short fuse. He looked over at Roger and Frank, who were feeding the dogs, and at Patty, who was arranging bird supplies. In the back, he could see Suzy cleaning the silk-screening equipment and Danny straightening up the stock.

"I could see the children in diapers raging against their lives in the basement of that school Corinne and I visited while we were still at the Bonaparte School," he recalled. "I remembered those warehoused in state institutions, where they were sometimes peddled like prostitutes. I was ready to launch a harangue, telling this snob about our special friends who were happy in their useful, meaningful lives. I wanted to tell her that the retarded were all over the world and that they needed her help. I was coming to a boil."

Patty plucked the woman's sleeve. Patty was one of the most socially developed. She was a pretty girl who spoke with a lilting, soft lisp.

"I'm one of them," she said to the woman.

♦ Chapter 4 ♦

The Lambs Pet Shop, State Street

On the way home, Bob pulled to the side of the road. He and Corinne prayed together. It helped, but the shock of the sudden dismissal was painful, especially for Corinne. "Three years of work," Corinne recalled in 1989. "We loved Hull House. Now it was gone. It was just before Christmas. I was so shaken that I could barely walk."

"I think we were set up," Corinne would say three decades later. "The director had our severance checks all ready. He wanted us out."

Many of the parents of Retarded Children's Aid were shocked when they heard of the firings. A number liked the idea of the pet store. "Why didn't you tell us?" they asked. "We have $8,000 in our treasury." RCA parents served as the trustees of the group and set policies. But the director had kept the parents in the dark. Only a few even knew of the proposed pet store.

It would be just over nine months from the day Bob and Corinne were fired until the opening of the Lambs Pet Shop at 913 North State Street on September 28, 1961. The period was filled with anxiety, failed efforts, and a great many small miracles.

The next day, Corinne and Bob returned to the Illinois Council on Mental Retardation. They wanted to visit the director, who had given them some earlier moral support.

61

They learned that she had left to take another job. They were introduced to her successor, who offered no encouragement at all. Years later, they would learn that, immediately after their visit, he sent a letter to all the mental retardation organizations in the area disassociating the Illinois Council from the Lambs and advising all others to do the same. As Bob recalled, "The letter described us as charlatans who were attempting to make money on the retarded." Little wonder that, even years after the Lambs Farm was a reality, professional people would walk away from Corinne and Bob after they introduced themselves at professional meetings.

They had to make a living. Bob still had his weekend railroad job. The Milwaukee Road put him back to work full-time. His wife, Mary Ruth, took a part-time job. Her parents lived with them and helped to look after the children.

Later the railroad would offer Bob an engineer's job paying nearly $18,000 annually with generous fringe benefits. He refused without hesitation, although afterward he wondered if he was being sensible or sane. When the store finally opened, Bob received $4,500 per year. The receipt books from that period show a take-home pay of $174.50 for two weeks' work. Corinne would receive even less—under $3,000 per year. The rationale at the time was that Bob was a head of household and that Corinne's husband, Trevor, was the main breadwinner in her family. Whatever the case, the eventual aim was to pay each of them the equivalent of a public school principal's salary, a goal they never reached on State Street. The entire Owen and Terese families sacrificed for many years to make the Lambs Pet Store a reality.

Corinne took a temporary job at a florist's, then sold subscriptions for *Life* magazine. Her mother lived with the Owens and took care of the three children.

In their spare time, Bob and Corinne continued their quest for the pet store.

Their first solicitation call was to L. Gifford Gardner, then owner and president of Pioneer Pet Supply in Oak Park, Illinois. It was a cold call—no appointment, no warning.

Corinne and Bob were inexperienced and naive in the ways of business. They thought that one dropped in as one would on a neighbor. Ironically, the style proved successful. Would-be benefactors were charmed by their simple, direct approach.

Gardner, now retired and living in Fort Myers, Florida, was guarded. He listened to their plan and was mildly skeptical.

Later, another friend, Bill Meyers, would be frank. "You're going to open up a pet shop?" he asked incredulously. "You? When you don't have any capital—or any experience with pets? When your whole work force is going to be retarded kids who haven't any experience with pets either? Brother, this is a disaster."

Like most people, Gardner knew little about the mentally retarded, and the notion of a business being staffed by them was completely new to him. "If you're just two teachers looking for a fast buck, you can forget it," he said. But he was so impressed by their sincerity that he told them, "Find a store; get it set up. Then come back, and we'll see what we can do."

Gardner was true to his word. Once the store was ready, he gave them almost $8,000 worth of supplies, much of it from his own warehouse and the remainder from other suppliers whom he had persuaded to help. The gift was all the more appreciated and meaningful because, at that time, the Lambs organization did not enjoy not-for-profit status.

Sometime during the first year, their attorney, George Van Emden, worked out an approach that would lead to a tax-exempt designation. It was a tough call. The Lambs organization, after all, was not a hospital or a church. Strictly speaking, it was not a school. It was, in fact, a store that hoped to make a profit. Although the profit would eventually accrue to the benefit of the Lambs by providing a home for them, in 1961 that was a difficult line to trace. It would take them until the following October, and in the interim, Giff Gardner and his friends could claim no deduction for their contributions. It was pure charity.

Van Emden was an invaluable friend. A good lawyer, he saw problems where they only cast a shadow, and thus brought some necessary realism to their thinking. They followed his advice most of the time, but when he insisted that two people could not be coequal directors, Bob and Corinne were equally insistent that they could work together. A prudent observer would have sided with the attorney, but magically the arrangement worked out better than many marriages.

Bob and Corinne were opposites in almost every way. Bob would be the sometimes impatient disciplinarian; Corinne would explain and mollify. During solicitation calls, Bob would state the facts and make the request; Corinne would talk about the Lambs themselves. Perhaps the only thing they did in unison was to pray together before making any decision or any solicitation call.

It was Van Emden who got them out of their first sticky legal situation. The Lambs store had barely become known when it received a lawyer's letter from the Lambs of New York, a fraternal theatrical association known for its many charities. An exchange of polite letters produced an agreement. The Lambs store would carry the scriptural legend "Feed My Lambs" on its masthead and proclaim its not-for-profit status. Corinne Owen, in particular, was delighted with the friendly settlement. "It's everything that we are," she observed.

Bob worked the midnight to 8:00 A.M. shift at the railroad, and Corinne solicited subscriptions from 9:00 to 1:00. The remainder of the day was spent calling on businesspeople, people in the pet supply industry, parents of the retarded—anyone who would listen. It was slow work. Most calls were dead ends. Bob and Corinne averaged no better than other solicitors—only about one in five prospects was interested.

Bob has a salesman's instincts and a flair for public relations. Part of it comes from a deep-seated belief in the value of what he is doing; part is an absolute trust that things will work out, a virtue he shares with Corinne. "We're not like other fund-raisers," he said. "Our jobs never depended upon a bottom line. If people didn't give, we simply went to the next call."

But he had a certain instinct about the calls to make. He knew how to network. A call to J. Chalmers O'Brien, a retired vice president of Carson Pirie Scott, a large Chicago department store, produced an introduction to Stuart List, publisher of the *Chicago American*. List promised publicity for the opening of the store. He introduced Bob and Corinne to Julie Ann Lyman of the *Chicago Tribune*, who later did a feature story for the Sunday *Tribune*.

List also introduced them to Clinton E. Frank, owner of an advertising agency and a producer of commercial films. Frank had been a football star at Yale and the third winner of the coveted Heisman Trophy in 1937. He was well known in Chicago. It was Frank who would later sponsor a thirty-minute movie narrated by actor Gary Merrill. Frank assigned Don Rutz to their account. Rutz eventually became an early member of the Lambs Farm's board of directors.

Again, not every call was successful. One man in the pet business, the father of a retarded child, refused to help. Others declined, suspecting that Corinne and Bob might be exploiting the retarded. Some businesspeople thought that, given the pool of cheap labor the retarded represented, they would undersell the competition. Giff Gardner had already advised the store to keep its prices in line with the competition. Bob and Corinne had every intention of doing so. The profits would build a home for the Lambs.

Gardner recalled the first efforts to find a suitable location for the store. "We were lucky," he said. "But if people had seen the horrible condition of the long-vacated cleaning store on State Street, they wouldn't have thought so."

Each of the parents on the then-informal board of the Lambs had donated $50 toward the rental of the store. In 1961, $50 represented a sacrificial gift. Few of the Lambs came from substantial homes. The gifts also prompted involvement, and each set of parents was convinced that they had found the ideal location for the pet shop. In no time,

Bob and Corinne had eight possibilities. The rents were competitive—about $200 to $225 per month—and virtually all the locations were in move-in condition.

They returned to Delilah White for advice. She had just relocated her apartment home to a new twin-towered building on the Chicago River called Marina Towers. She spoke to William McFetridge, one of the contractors for the new building. He assigned his secretary to explore the area. Not long after, Delilah received a letter from McFetridge informing her that there was a store available at 913 North State Street. He also included his personal check for $500, a major gift in those days.

The store had been a Magikist rug-cleaning facility. It looked as if it had been bombed. The floor was covered with debris and cratered where the previous tenants had secured their massive rug-cleaning machines. Steam from the machines had soaked and flaked the wall right down to the brickwork. The toilet bowls were cracked, the water heater had been ripped out, and there was a hole in the roof where the air conditioner had been. They were to learn later that the roof was little more than tarpaper.

The landlord asked for rent of $350 per month—"the same as Magikist has been paying me," he added. Corinne and Bob were appalled. Minnie Allen, one of the mothers, said in desperation, "Where the hell are we gonna get that kind of money?" The eight other places they had seen were at least $100 less expensive and were in move-in condition.

"Forget the condition of the place," Delilah White told them. "Just look at this location!" They were only two blocks from the city's famous Gold Coast and in the middle of a densely populated area of largely high-income people. "Look at all those people inside those high rises," Delilah said. "Think of all those poodles and cats."

They had thought about poodles and cats, but the advice they had received was to stay away from them. When they told the irrepressible Delilah, she countered, "Well, you'll have the supplies for them. And you can have birds or fish. People in high rises are lonely for pets, and there isn't a pet store within miles of here."

The parents were shocked at the condition of the store as well as its price. They understood the desirable location but were still pressing for the various locations they had found. In desperation, Bob tossed the names in a hat. "Honest to God—and don't tell me He didn't have something to do with it—we pulled out 913 North State Street."

Corinne and Bob credit such happenings to their frequent prayers. Each day, after they parked the car, they would pause for a moment's prayer as they crossed the famous Bughouse Square, a park once famous for its soapbox orators. Each day, they recalled, "We told the Lord that He had to put it together."

The location was settled, but the financial situation was worsened by the higher rent. Corinne and Bob decided to call upon William Gage, president of Magikist, and ask him for two months' free rent. Although Magikist had vacated the store, it still held the lease. Gage gave them five months and later extended it to six.

Why did he give a half-year's free rent to two people with no official affiliation, no office, no tax-exempt status—literally nothing? Years later, journalist Jim Poling, writing about the Lambs' community for the *Ladies' Home Journal*, interviewed Gage, who said, "Well, you know, I get hundreds of requests for contributions. And everyone who calls me or comes in tells me how many people I'll be helping and exactly what my money's going to do. Bob and Corinne were so honest and sincere. They were only helping a few—twelve kids—and they had a thousand different things to do. They weren't going to put up a Bill Gage counter or a Bill Gage floor. They didn't know what they'd do with the money I'd saved them—but that's just why I gave it to them. They needed it so badly."

The next months were a blur of activity. Bob and Corinne still had their jobs. They spent their afternoons begging for money and materials. Mike Hansen of the Fair Department Store (later sold to another chain) turned over his carpenters and his decorating department; Sid and Bill Meyers of the Chicago Bird and Cage Company contributed materials from their stock; Tony Menotti, a heating contractor whom Bob had met through his uncle, installed a new plumbing and heating system. He charged only cost for the heating units; all else was a gift. Menotti was not a big contractor at that time. His gift was a truly sacrificial one. Without it, the fragile project could have been aborted. At that time, the Lambs were down to their last $200.

When the 600-square-foot sales space was ready, Gifford Gardner assigned one of his best salesmen, Al Masuto, to help out. Masuto went to the store with his father and set it up according to the best sales principles. It looked like a quality pet store. It was.

Jewel Foods, a large supermarket chain, offered some used shopping gondolas (moving shelves). Bob rushed to Pioneer Pet Supply and borrowed a truck, loaded the gondolas, and delivered them to the store. It was the first time he had used the young Lambs to help with a major task. They had been helping with the painting, unpacking, and shelving. Now, however, they were "going out"—doing things that ordinary people did. The hurried experience was a hint of what they could and would be encouraged to do.

By the end of August 1961, only some cabinet work and electrical wiring needed to be done. The light fixtures had been donated by Clarke Robertson, the father of one of the Lambs. A stockbroker, Robertson had a large network of friends. His brother was a U.S. congressman, and Clarke was a close friend of Joseph Meek, another former congressman and the president of the State Street Council. It was Clarke Robertson who had introduced them to Chalmers O'Brien.

Getting the place wired was a study in frustration. Not every volunteer was true to his word. The promised electrician never showed up. The work was completed almost on the eve of the opening.

The opening was a great success. The window was filled with pet supplies. There were twenty tanks stocked with tropical fish. There were canaries, turtles, hamsters—even a wandering raccoon named Sweetie. Three years of hope had come true. Twelve young Lambs, their parents, and an assortment of friends filled the store.

The store's salesroom looked like a circus tent. There were red awnings over the shelves and against the side walls. The back wall was painted like a circus with three rings of animals. The gondolas in the middle of the floor were stocked.

Media coverage was modest but more than any small-business owner could hope for. The *Chicago American*, now defunct, covered the event. Channel 7, the local ABC outlet, sent its reporter-at-large, the late Alex Dreier, to do a brief human-interest piece. It made the 10:00 P.M. news, and the young Lambs were thrilled.

There was punch and cookies. Sweetie the raccoon—a gift of Charlie Hume, a friend who raised experimental animals for laboratories—stole the show with her rhinestone collar. It was a fine opening, but by 11:00 A.M. the crowd was gone, and the store stood ready for customers. With a staff of fourteen—twelve Lambs and Corinne and Bob—it may have been the most overstaffed store in Chicago. But there were no customers.

Bob approached the cash register. In mock tones, he ordered a box of dog Yummies. Corinne had one of the Lambs get the box while Bob pulled forty-nine cents from his pocket. The cash register rang.

Nine months after Corinne and Bob had been fired from RCA, the Lambs Pet Shop had made its first sale.

◆ Lambs Tales ◆
Howard

Not every story of the Lambs is a happy one—and not all involve the mentally disabled.

Nearly fifty calls to a man who had volunteered to install the electrical fixtures had produced nothing. One day a young man wandered in. He was about thirty, clean shaven, articulate. His clothes had seen better days, but he was presentable. He said his name was Howard and that he could use some work. When he told Bob that he had done some electrical work while in the U.S. Navy, he seemed a dream come true. Further, he was willing to work for all the store could offer—the minimum wage of about $1.25 per hour.

He was true to his word. The fixtures were up in time for the opening. When the pet store opened, Corinne and Bob found that they needed Howard. They were so busy teaching their charges that they often had no time for basic maintenance and for running errands. Howard was perfect.

The Lambs liked Howard. In the months that followed, they came to know and enjoy him. From the little he told them, he had had a hard life. The retarded do not always fully understand the chemistry of complex relationships, but they respond exceptionally well to feelings. It is almost as if they can read souls.

Howard was kind to them. He shared their interest in animals. He lived in a room not far from the store and would go on Sundays, when the store was closed, to feed the animals.

On Christmas Eve, Danny, one of the Lambs, came to Corinne. He quietly showed her a necktie—a gift for Howard—that the twelve Lambs had all chipped in to buy. When they presented it to him, he was so moved that he purchased a dozen Christmas cards—one for each of them.

At the close of business each day, the Lambs were careful to bank their receipts. They left only $35 in the cash drawer for the next day. When the store opened on the day after Christmas, Bob Terese found the cash drawer empty. In its place was a note from Howard, apologizing for the theft and asking forgiveness. He said that he hadn't been able to stop himself.

The Lambs tried to find him. They wanted to help him, not punish him. But he had vanished into the big city. They saw him only once more. They called out to him, but he ran away.

◆ Chapter 5 ◆

The Lambs in Business

Romance gave way to reality. Two teachers and twelve young retarded adults were running a business—one that none of them knew anything about. They had twenty fish tanks and no experience with feeding tropical fish. Corinne would arrive each morning worried about how many fish were floating on top of the tanks. Only four of the Lambs could count. Bob had to do the shopping. He and Corinne needed to be out in the community, telling the Lambs' story. Most important, during the first month, almost no one came into the store. Understandably, the parents were concerned.

When the Lambs organization was established as a corporate entity, policy decisions were vested in the board of directors. Bob and Corinne were considered employees, at an initial salary of $300 per month each. The founders wanted it that way. They had already witnessed the personal profits being made by owner-managers of other facilities for the handicapped.

A number of these places provided quality custodial care for the retarded. Their clients were well looked after, but they showed no growth. They were taught basic social graces and given what amounted to play therapy. Because of the high tuition these facilities charged, it would not be appropriate to expect them to work.

Even some parents of the retarded fall victim to such

muddled thinking. Although they expect a measure of work in the household from their other children, they ask nothing from the retarded member of the family—resulting in even more deterioration of the retarded family member.

Finally, the costs incurred in such enterprises ensured that only children from wealthy families could be accepted.

Bob and Corinne were determined that their vision would not be blurred by concern over monies. Monthly tuition would be $15. The parents would have legal and fiscal control. Technically, they could fire the very people who had inspired the enterprise—a policy that would be sorely tested in years to come.

The sales policy established at the State Street store would apply to all the organization's businesses. It said that all business interests would be subordinate to the interests of the Lambs. The puppies in the window at the Lambs Pet Store, for example, were there primarily for the education and emotional well-being of the members of the Lambs' community. The puppies were to be sold at a profit but only to support further efforts on behalf of the Lambs.

This philosophy resulted in an even more idealistic sales policy than that of the legendary merchandiser Marshall Field, who coined the phrase: "Give the lady what she wants." At the Lambs Pet Store, no return of merchandise was ever questioned. Although they sometimes knew that they were being taken advantage of, the Lambs always cheerfully took back animals and merchandise, a policy still in effect at the Lambs Farm. Without it, the organization could readily have lost its focus.

The original twelve Lambs ranged in age from eighteen to thirty-three. Their mental age was roughly between seven and ten years. The six females and six males always dressed well. (Bob and Corinne insisted on this, even risking parental ire by sending one young woman home when she arrived dressed in what they considered a slovenly manner. "She looked awful," Corinne said. "Dressed like a butcher. We told her that she couldn't clerk at Marshall Field's dressed like that, so she couldn't do it here.")

The Lambs were charming ambassadors of goodwill—ideal for sales. Always willing to please, they sometimes got in over their heads by promising customers what they could not deliver. But for many of the customers, this was the only indication of their limitations. Further, they alleviated deep-seated fears. ("Will they hurt me?" a customer asked Corinne one day. It sounded laughable, but it was a measure of the thinking in vogue at the time. "No," Corinne answered, "you can buy any of our dogs with confidence.")

After several potential customers came in thinking they were at a hardware store, Bob went against the advice of the marketing professionals and began putting animals in the window. Before this, the window had been stocked with pet supplies and empty fish tanks. The display could readily have been mistaken for that of a hardware or seed supply store. The doggie-in-the-window strategy paid off. Gradually, people began to recognize that it was a pet store.

The store drew mixed reactions, some of them difficult to trace. U.S. Senator Adlai Stevenson and his wife, Nancy, came in weekly with their children. Members of the famous Wrigley family, owners of the chewing gum conglomerate and the Chicago Cubs, who play their games at Wrigley Field, were occasional customers. Clusters of the extended Pritzker family, said to be Chicago's first billionaires, shopped there for their pet supply needs.

Yet, during the store's entire first year on State Street, not a single student from the large public elementary school across the street visited the store. Fear and distrust of the retarded appear to be inculcated early. Perhaps the most loving and trusting people in society, the retarded are often unwittingly described by parents of normal children as somehow mentally ill or sinister. Often, parents will inform their children that another child is retarded without explaining what retardation means. Sadly, the message the child receives is a negative one, replete with fears. Soon the term *retarded* is translated into one of derision in the school yard. The die is cast.

When customers began to come, Bob and Corinne tried to

ensure that no customers left the store without learning something about the Lambs. "We wanted them to know what we were doing," he said, "and why we felt that what we were doing was worthwhile." They drew the line, however, at placing any signs in the window or on the walls indicating that the shop was run for the benefit of the retarded. They felt that this would be exploitation.

The policy is still in place today. The highway sign that advertises the Lambs Farm, the welcome sign at its entrance, the Country Inn and Store—nothing announces retarded adults. Having come out of attics, basements, and gray institutional dormitories, the Lambs would not be put back in.

For Corinne and Bob, managing the store always meant a six-day week, twelve to fourteen hours a day. Part of this work load had to do with training their retarded associates; much of it was simply the realities of managing what amounted to a mom-and-pop business. Bob was constantly making calls to secure contributions or to attract much-needed publicity. Both would often travel to homes, meeting halls, and church basements to tell the story of the Lambs— often to other interested parents of retarded children. They would travel twenty-five miles to talk to ten people.

It took time, but the investment would pay off. Business at the store improved, and years later, many of their early listeners came to the Farm to enjoy a meal at the Country Inn.

After almost a year, the Lambs themselves gradually developed a sense of proprietorship in the store. After nearly a lifetime of passive dependence and acceptance, they needed endless coaxing to instill a sense of belonging. Gradually, they learned to perform tasks without being asked. They began to straighten shelves, to pick things up. They absorbed the rhythms of the store.

Part of the process was aided by Bob and Corinne's determined effort to treat the Lambs as partners, not employees. Corinne, in particular, could speak to them as a friend and not as a teacher. Bob was inclined to be more directive. (When one new Lamb told another how much he liked Mr. Terese, an older veteran smiled and said, "I hope you still like him when he yells at you." Bob later explained, "You don't really yell at retarded people. But a lot of discipline is acting.")

Learning to relate to the retarded is a process. After over three decades of such a process, Corinne and Bob—together with many other long-time staffers at the Lambs Farm—have so erased the emotional barriers to communication that they appear unaware that they are interacting with mentally handicapped persons. (In interviews for this history, Lambs Farm staffers often became nonplussed when questions were raised about communication. "They're people. Just people. People like us," they answered.)

The process of flattening out—this gradual erosion of artificial barriers between normal and retarded people—may be best exemplified by Corinne Owen, who appears to have come by it naturally. "Oh, I did a dumb thing," she will say, having misplaced something. "Don't do that, Mary. That's stupid," she will say. Her language isn't guarded, because it isn't judgmental. She isn't trying to "get down to their level"; she simply refuses to acknowledge any of the stereotypical attitudes that hinder communication.

The store attracted fewer than a dozen customers each day. Those ten- and fifteen-dollar days proved a mixed blessing. Bob was able to learn the hard lessons of marketing a small business; Corinne had a certain amount of time away from the cash register to train the dozen partners in the enterprise.

Steve Buell was one of the first members of the group. His father, who would later buy thousands of greeting cards from the Lambs for his *Popular Mechanics* magazine, donated a conference table from the magazine's Chicago offices. It became Corinne's teaching table.

Since only four of the twelve Lambs could read with any facility, they had to be taught to sight-read. New merchandise was sorted on the table. Corinne would ask the Lambs to find the product on the shelves. She turned it into a game. Gradually, they learned to distinguish one product from another, one brand from another.

Then they learned to count. While some could recite numbers, they were unable to connect them with individual units. Thus, while reciting "one, two, three," they would push three or four boxes of birdseed with each number they recited. It took time to get some of them to associate one number with one unit. It took even longer to teach them how many boxes of a given product were needed to stock a shelf.

Pricing merchandise was even more difficult. Some Lambs needed to be taught to recognize the symbols and then to write them. Then Corinne had to ensure that the Lambs put the symbols in proper order on the merchandise. From time to time, some would invert the numbers, thus turning a thirty-nine-cent product into a ninety-three-cent item. Price increases, which were frequent in those inflationary days, could make for enormous difficulty. The retarded tend to be brittle about making changes; this tested even Corinne's seemingly unlimited patience.

As early as their days at the Bonaparte School, Corinne and Bob had recognized the varying strengths and weaknesses of their students. This understanding was reinforced by their three years' experience at RCA. Now, however, in a functionally tutorial situation, the variation became even more apparent.

In the average school setting, academic weaknesses are uncovered, and the teacher then focuses on each weakness until it is corrected. These young adults needed a completely opposite tack. Pointing out weaknesses in the mentally disabled would only lower their already fragile self-image. Bob and Corinne focused on strengths. Danny, for example, was good at putting things away and had a good sense of direction. He was placed in charge of the storeroom and, later, made deliveries.

The teaching-from-strengths approach was not without its drawbacks. Some well-meaning parents insisted that their children could do more complex tasks. Others wanted their children to do tasks they witnessed other retarded people doing, forgetting that their son or daughter had a low ability level or different skills.

One father, for example, was incensed that his son was put to work cleaning puppy cages. He wanted the son handling sales and working the register, two tasks for which he was profoundly underqualified. Repeated appeals to the father's good sense only angered him more. So the young man was put to work at the sales counter. The stress seemed so much for him that he suffered a minor breakdown. The still angry father withdrew him from the program.

The vast majority of parents, however, supported every phase of the process. At first, Bob Terese's mother acted as volunteer secretary to the enterprise, typing letters dictated to her over the phone. Later, mothers of the Lambs themselves volunteered to type. Soon some were contributing a day a week in the store, working the cash register, to free Corinne for teaching and Bob for promotions. Patty's mother began to make butter cookies for the Lambs. The cookies later became one of the most famous products at the Lambs Farm's country store. (Patty, a member of the pioneer group, remains a member of the Lambs' community. She is a valued employee of the Grove School, a facility for the severely retarded and physically handicapped.)

The silk-screening was already under way when the Ceramics Guild donated some $1,500 worth of ceramics equipment. The guild even contributed two teachers—Bea Czerny and Eileen Kane. The students liked the work; it filled the spaces between store-related activities. However, they had difficulty with the glazing, and the teachers could come only one afternoon per week. Bob and Corinne knew little about glazing, so eventually the project had to be abandoned. Later the equipment would be used to glaze silk-screened tile at the Lambs Farm.

Teaching the retarded requires patience and some inverted thinking. "They don't respond to yelling," Corinne said. "They respond to positive reinforcement. There is nothing they want more than to please you."

"Once you yell at the retarded," Bob said, "they just dig in their heels, and you can't do anything with them." It is a lesson that might well apply to normal people.

"When they come into the program," Bob recalled, "they are filled wih apprehension. Our staff often has to redo their whole spirit." It has been that way since the early days at the pet shop. After nearly five years of working with these special-needs people, Bob and Corinne were forming a deeper understanding of them. They were learning from their clients. "If I didn't learn from them," Bob said, "I would never have been able to teach them."

Slowly, the Lambs began to thrive in the environment of a store they had come to think of as their own. They formed a community that became so strong that it rivaled that of their own families. When one parent told her son of a Christmas party date that conflicted with one of the early Lambs' Christmas parties, the young man announced that he was going to the Lambs' party.

By the spring of 1965, less than four years after the store's opening, its bank account showed a balance of $20,000. The profit was unimpressive for some forty-two months in business. However, the primary purpose of the venture was not to make a profit. Twelve Lambs—the number would grow to twenty-two—were learning something about dignity, self-worth, and responsibility. They were growing. They were happy.

It wasn't all roses. There were conflicts. One young woman had to be separated from the program. The entire group had to be disciplined when Bob and Corinne learned that they had been hustling free sodas and coffee for more than a year from Jim Sain, the owner of a local restaurant. Bob and Corinne had their inevitable differences about approaches to training. "We used to fight in the car," Corinne said, "but we always presented a united front with the Lambs."

There were moments of laughter, like the time an eccentric, wealthy lady asked the Lambs to "baby-sit" her monkey. She sent the creature over by taxi. Before the end of the day, it escaped from its box and roamed the store, knocking over everything in sight. Someone called the police; six officers soon arrived. Alonzo, the clever spider monkey, eluded them all. Eventually animal experts from Chicago's Lincoln Park Zoo were needed to corral the overactive monkey.

There were hard-won lessons. The Lambs' skin thickened a bit when a well-dressed man parked his Mercedes in front of the shop, then purchased a puppy and virtually everything a wealthy dog could use. It was a major sale—until the check bounced.

Most important, the Lambs were learning responsibility. When Bob Terese took his first vacation in 1964, Corinne was concerned that the young people would take advantage of her gentle nature while Bob was away. The experience proved just the opposite. Bob recalled, "They went out of their way to help her while I was gone. They not only did their own chores but asked her repeatedly what other tasks they could do."

And they learned caring. From their own meager budget, they were sending gifts to other retarded people—those institutionalized at the state facility at Dixon, Illinois. Some of them had lived at Dixon in the 1950s. Vastly improved now, the institution was then viewed as a last resort. The Lambs bought transistor radios with their modest budget and sent them to their less fortunate friends at Dixon.

When they learned of the efforts of the Gold Coast Lions Club to raise money for the blind, the Lambs wanted to join in. One of the special missions of the Lambs organization is to raise funds for the visually impaired. The Lions promised to match the Lambs' efforts, sharing their collected funds with them. It was an incentive that energized the eager young people even more. Taking their begging cans supplied by the Lions, the Lambs covered all the corners and shopping areas in the vicinity of the store. Partly because they were now well known to the area's residents and partly because of their persistence, they collected more money to aid the blind than any other group. Dressed in their yellow hats and jackets and giving away the famous Tootsie Rolls donated to the Lions, they built more confidence in themselves, meeting people away from the security of the store.

"Our biggest asset was always the Lambs themselves," Bob said. "They sold themselves. They could make friends with people." When weather permitted, they would put their deodorized pet skunk on a leash and walk him outside the store. People stopped, stared, and talked to the Lambs. Barriers fell.

New members came to the Lambs' community, many through referrals by Delilah White. She continued to evaluate and screen all applicants and to encourage the organization's efforts. Always something of a maverick, she continued to insist that IQ was not the sole measure of a child's development and, further, that IQ performance can be improved. Such thinking ran counter to established theory, which held that an IQ is a fixed number, especially for the retarded. She and her Levenson Center remained outside the pale, while educators pointed to the dated research from which they derived their fixed views.

For the Lambs' program, she remained an energetic supporter. Years before, her own vision for what became Little City in Palatine, Illinois, had included plans for a flower shop, a gas station, a post office, and other services. She left Little City before her dream could be realized, but the ideas were still stirring in her mind, and she saw a possibility of recreating them through the Lambs organization. (Little City survived and flourished. While Delilah White's ideas found a more receptive home at the Lambs Farm, the Little City community, which cares for several hundred more severely retarded adults, has become one of the model facilities in the country.)

However, as the Lambs became better known, word-of-mouth applicants arrived, largely through Bob's public relations efforts. He has an intuitive public relations sense. He can plant a story, largely because he so believes in the mission of the Lambs that he is unafraid to ask. Chicago columnists Jack Mabley (who was a good customer), Maggie Daly,

Irv Kupcinet, and Herb Lyons often gave them plugs in their bullet-paragraphed, three-dot columns.

In 1962, Julie Ann Lyman did a full-length feature on the store in the *Chicago Tribune*'s Sunday magazine. Bob had planted the story with Bill McFetridge. It was a public relations dream come true. The spin-offs were wonderful. ABC-TV did an evening feature on Channel 7; Mal Bellairs, interviewer for WBBM, a major radio station, did a story; WIND, another megawatt station, virtually adopted the Lambs. A local religious station, WMBI, based at the Moody Bible Institute, featured the Lambs Pet Store on its "Bob Murfin in the Morning" show. Bob and Corinne were invited to Don McNeil's famous "Breakfast Club," which was broadcast nationally. Several nights each week, Corinne and Bob would take their dog and pony shows before fraternal groups such as the Rotary, Lions, and Elks.

Corinne Owen, with several of the Lambs and a colorful toucan, staffed a booth at Chicago's annual Flower Show, held at McCormick Place. The toucan, named DeGaulle, was practically the shop logo. Although it was for sale, the Lambs hated to part with it. Eventually, it was sold not once, but three times. People paid $250 for the colorful bird but kept bringing it back. DeGaulle, it seems, preferred the companionship of the Lambs. Sales at the Flower Show were negligible, but the exposure to thousands of socially active ladies brought even more recognition.

The booth attempted to sell turtles and chameleons. Even Corinne was queasy about handling chameleons. The white-gloved ladies winced at the lizardlike creatures. They screamed when dozens of them escaped from their box and when they witnessed the toucan with one in his powerful beak. "Look at that lady," they screamed. "She's feeding chameleons to her bird!"

By the time Bob arrived to pick up Corinne, she was beside herself. "Let me tell you something," Corinne seethed. "Chameleons bite!" Her wrists were covered with small bite marks.

Chicago's mayor, the late Richard J. Daley, came to the

Lambs' booth and purchased a couple of jars of jam, which the Lambs had begun to sell. The powerful mayor's presence amounted to another endorsement.

By 1964, the Lambs' community had grown unwieldy. There were now twenty-two Lambs, staffing a sales area of only 600 square feet. They were bumping into each other. There simply was not enough work to keep them busy.

Bob and Corinne put them on morning and afternoon shifts. The decision was very unpopular with the Lambs, who loved being in the store. They had boundless energy and had formed deep friendships with each other. The new schedule separated Suzy and Johnny, for example, who had fallen in love. Johnny insisted on staying for the second shift in order to be with Suzy. It got sticky. Words flew. Bob issued his famous dictum: "Out the door!" Bob and Corinne weren't trying to wreck a romance, only to run a store. They told Johnny that he'd have to see Suzy on his own time.

Something had to be done about the overcrowding and underemployment. They tried a sheltered-workshop contract. "We packaged pea shooters, of all things," Corinne recalled. "It got to be so big a job that we had to hire an assistant. But she couldn't count any better than the Lambs. So we gave it up."

The Lambs had learned a great deal in three years. A number of them were clearly prepared for outside employment. Further, they could earn more at outside jobs. Their salaries at the Lambs amount to a pittance. Some earned only $10 per month, lower than the minimum wage. It was a token salary. They could have been paid more, but the dream of a residential community for the Lambs would never have become a reality.

Bob approached an early adviser, Chalmers O'Brien, the retired vice president of Carson Pirie Scott, about the possibility of part-time work for some of the Lambs. O'Brien referred him to Fred Englund, then the director of personnel at the large department store.

Englund was cautious. Carson's had a good reputation in the area for risk hiring. The company had earned praise for its policy of employing school dropouts and giving them a second chance. Carson's had hired only one retarded adult to unload trucks on the night shift and was having trouble with him because he kept falling asleep on the job. However, after Bob had placed Judy and John in Meyer's Pet Shop in Carson's and Carol in Amlings Flowerland, another franchise within the department store, Englund decided to take a risk. Danny was hired as a stock boy; Jerry, in the china department. In a very short time, five of the Lambs were employed in the Carson's complex.

The openings at Carson's were the start of an outside-employment system that became an integral part of the Lambs' program. It was the beginning of what is now known as the Vocational Department. Today, this department is staffed by four people and provides training and job opportunities for virtually all the Lambs. Over thirty Lambs are currently working in competitive jobs off the Farm.

In 1989, Lambs working outside the Farm complex earned over $300,000, not including benefits and stock options. Now a successful, professionally run operation, the Vocational Department was born of need, a phone call, and the persistent salesmanship of Bob Terese.

The first Lambs to take the risk fared well. Danny, the stockroom clerk at Carson's, went on to full-time employment at Amlings Flowerland. Still later, with the help of his parents, he opened his own newsstand on the corner of Irving Park and Pulaski.

Carol flourished at Amlings. She had never liked working with pets. At one point, Bob and Corinne began potting and selling plants, largely to provide Carol with something she liked. She had a gift for arranging flowers. The experience helped her to overcome her fear of failure.

John and Judy worked out well at Meyer's Pet Shop. Later John found full-time employment in the maintenance department at the post office. But personal problems in Judy's family eventually put a strain on her ability to work at the store.

Dennis applied for full-time work at Carson's. It proved more than he could handle, so he returned to the Lambs Farm, by then in Libertyville, and took charge of the commuting program.

Jerry did well in Carson's china department, remaining part-time and keeping his link with the Lambs. He is still employed at Carson's and is also a volunteer in the sheltered workshop at the Lambs Farm.

Although the outside work program was a success, it did not relieve the pressure of employee overload at the store. Bob and Corinne still had four or five people more than they needed and were under increasing pressure to accept more. The split shifts weren't working well. The Lambs simply wouldn't go home. Even when the store hired a night manager, Ron Pierce, a young man from the Moody Bible Institute, and began to remain open evenings until seven to accommodate working people, there were still too many Lambs to train or employ effectively.

After four years, the treasury of the Lambs Pet Store had a balance of $25,000. The program had reached a saturation point. The board of directors discussed branching out—opening additional pet shops in the Chicago suburbs, but this would have caused them to delay the dream of a community for the Lambs.

It was time to move on.

The Lambs, the Bunny, and the Mob

Chicago has been described as the city with the beautiful front yard and the dirty backyard. This rather simplified description contains a particle of truth.

Less than a five-minute walk from the Lambs Pet Store on State Street is the city's Gold Coast. Its posh stores sell the latest fashions at stratospheric prices. A condominium with a view can cost upwards of a million dollars. Just behind the facade, however, are some run-down tenements, tawdry nightclubs and bars, grubby stores, and hot dog joints. In the evening, the city's famous Rush Street area, just two short blocks from State Street, caters to the needs of a broad spectrum of people. Drugs are easy to find. So are prostitutes. Some of the businesses are little more than cash registers for mob interests, who launder their ill-gotten monies through a tacky restaurant front or jewelry store.

Bughouse Square, two short blocks away and just across from the famous Newberry Library, was once a platform for outdoor speakers. When television replaced the soapbox, the attractive park became a haven for prostitutes of both sexes and for down-and-outers of all stripes. The police try to keep things under control, but some cops are crooked, and some politicians are for sale at lower prices than the Michigan Avenue shoes. It's an interesting mix.

Yet the area is dotted with churches, schools, and universities. Corinne Owen called it "a very religious" area. She was right. However, sin nestles side by side with salvation.

Initially, some parents were genuinely concerned about the safety of the area for the Lambs, most of whom took city transportation to arrive at the shop.

The Lambs never had a problem. Indeed, other small-business owners, police, and private citizens came to know them and be protective of them. But the store brought in a wide variety of characters, including a man who wanted a white mouse on a leash and a number of people who had crossed the emotional line to live in the world of their pets. Perhaps loneliness is the cause of such behavior, but the Lambs had their share of customers who cared more for contact with a dog or a cat than for human companionship.

After months of orientation, the Lambs began to feel confident and at home in the store. At first, four—later six—Lambs were given keys to the store. The keys were symbols of real progress. For each Lamb, the key symbolized confidence. The Lambs were no longer viewed as charges to be supervised. The holders of the keys were so pleased that they began arriving upwards of a half-hour before Corinne and Bob each morning.

When Corinne and Bob arrived one morning, they found the door open. The Lambs were all gathered near the dog cages and being strangely quiet. (Developmentally disabled people tend to be verbal. To the unpracticed ear, they can sound loud, especially in groups.)

They were all looking toward the front of the store. When Bob and Corinne turned in that direction, they saw the object of the Lambs' attention: a young woman, sitting on the windowsill, cradling a dachshund puppy in her arms—and crying softly.

The Lambs whispered that they had found her outside the store when they arrived. She asked if she could come into the store with them. "Something bad must have happened," Danny said. "She's been crying since she came in."

Bob suggested lamely that she might simply be cold—a

flabby evasion, since it was summer, and the temperature was already in the sixties. "Cold?" Patty asked. "Maybe. Because under her coat, she's *naked!*"

She was a beautiful woman, long-legged, well groomed. Corinne looked closer. She wasn't naked; she was scantily costumed. "I think she's a Bunny," Corinne said. "Look at her stockings."

Bob Terese *was* looking. She was stunning. And then he saw another Bunny trademark, the black satin outfit with the white stand-up collar and bow tie.

Not long before, Hugh Hefner had founded his Playboy empire just a few blocks from the store. One of his clubs was located there. The smiling Bunnies served drinks to the self-absorbed club members, permitting them to feel sinful without actually sinning. The look-but-don't-touch rule was strictly enforced, and in the early days, the Bunnies used pseudonyms. The practice was supposed to protect them from unwanted advances, but it only served to diminish their self-concept even more. It was as if they were trained pets.

On this day, the scantily clad visitor simply sat there, absorbing the puppy's unconditional love. "Should I get her some coffee or a Coke?" Dennis asked. "No, leave her alone," Corinne said. "I think all she needs is a little privacy."

"If you ask me," Patty whispered, "all she really needs is a little love. Look at the way she's hugging that puppy."

She had come to the right place. Puppies exude love. Retarded people have the gift of unfiltered emotions—and emotional wisdom that seems to compensate for their intellectual shortcomings. They instinctively respected her need to be alone. They stood caringly, respecting her privacy.

"It's this quiet affection, this trust and faith in other people, that we have always found particularly appealing in the Lambs," Bob Terese wrote in 1970. "These people are really a blessing. All they want is love—the love that demonstrates care, concern, interest. In return, they will give you far more love than any normal child."

After a while, the Bunny quietly returned the puppy to its cage and slipped silently from the store.

Mr. G was different. He used the Lambs for his own purposes.

Mr. G had a retarded daughter who was nearly blind. "She was a very sweet, very quiet girl, willing to try anything the Lambs could do for her," recalled Bob. In spite of being 80 percent blind, she learned to stock shelves and do other tasks quite well. Her parents showed considerable interest. Her father, especially, visited the store at least three times each week—always solicitous and always leaving change for a few phone calls he made each time he came.

Sometimes, when Corinne and Bob arrived in the morning, Mr. G would be at the back of the store, talking in muffled tones on the phone. It seemed strange, but the Lambs' community didn't deal in suspicion.

One day, Mr. G told Bob that he had rented the vacant store next door. He was going to open a jewelry boutique for his wife. "Wouldn't it be great," he said, "if we could cut a door through the wall? Then we could visit our daughter all the time."

Bob hesitated. The door opened to the store's phone. He put Mr. G off.

A month later, his vague suspicions were confirmed. As he watched the evening news, Mr. G's picture flashed on the screen. He was about to be questioned by the Illinois Crime Commission—something to do with the juice-loan racket. It was obvious now. Mr. G was using the pet store's phone for his collection business.

Corinne saw the news, as did many of the other parents. The next day one of the board members resigned. He wanted Mr. G and his daughter out of the program.

The parental link threatened one of the cornerstones of the program. Lambs would be accepted solely on the basis of their potential to profit from the program. There were no tests other than age—a lower limit of sixteen, which was later raised to twenty-one. There was no race, creed, or color test, and no financial test. Those who could paid upwards of $25 per month; some paid nothing.

Corinne and Bob visited Stuart List, their close friend and adviser at the *Chicago American*. He agreed completely that Mr. G's daughter should remain in the program, no matter what the pressure from some parents. He suggested that Bob level with Mr. G.

When Bob told him that his phone privileges had terminated, Mr. G shrugged. "Bob," he said, "why don't you take a walk down the street to that nice custom shirt shop? Get yourself fitted for a dozen nice shirts, and tell them to put the shirts on my tab."

It could hardly have been a less appropriate bribe. Bob remains completely indifferent to clothes. He told Mr. G that he didn't need any shirts and that the phone was off limits.

His daughter left the program soon after. The Lambs were moving to Libertyville, and Mr. G said that he wouldn't be able to get her there. Shortly after, her eyesight grew worse. She was placed in an institution.

The Lambs' community had gained some valuable insights at a time when the organization was still fragile. The Lambs had weathered their first serious board crisis. The beautiful Bunny may have learned something about real caring. Mr. G taught the Lambs to be wary.

The dream survived.

◆ Interlude ◆
Corinne's Curriculum

"Our young people love to be useful but hate to be used."

Corinne Owen speaks so softly that some words escape even normal hearing. She is so small that she must have many of her clothes tailored. She has never learned to drive a car, a situation that has often required complex commuting arrangements. To the casual viewer, she is the stereotypical grandmother, especially when she walks into the Lambs Country Inn carrying one of the many flower-painted tin "pails" she favors as a pocketbook. Her co-founder, Bob Terese, has said often that, in their over thirty years of association, he has never seen her hurt anyone. In another setting, she could be described as a female Mr. Chips.

Such a portrait, however correct, presents only half the picture. Beneath the self-effacing exterior, there is a master teacher who knows her subject and passionately desires to impart it.

This drive may have come from her father. He wanted very much to preach but never had a parish of his own. He often preached at missions on West Madison Street, which was then the main street of Chicago's skid row. However, his need to work in order to support his family kept him from the pulpit.

He compensated by giving Corinne talks on Sunday afternoons. His talks, intended to inspire as well as discipline, often lasted over two hours. Although always a deeply religious woman, she regarded the talks as a punishment. "They upset me terribly," she said six decades later. But they might have taught her more patience than theology.

Clearly, her education and her teaching, almost exclusively in a tutorial setting, provided a structure on which she built her teaching program at the Lambs Pet Store and later the Farm. Later, too, she would discover some useful methodology in the reading program she sold door-to-door and would develop her natural powers of persuasiveness selling magazine subscriptions over the telephone.

What emerged from her long years of pre-Lambs experience was an ability to communicate knowledge that would form the heart of the special curriculum at the Lambs Farm. Years later, when the Lambs organization was applying for accreditation by the Commission on Accreditation of Retardation Facilities, Corinne Owen's now-standard teaching procedures and work manuals were submitted as part of the professional documentation.

"No one is perfect and especially not our young people," the manual reads. "Your strength as teacher lies in quietly and persistently keeping the work pattern and not becoming too upset if things are not always perfect."

Corinne Owen's teaching methods can most likely be found in any good pedagogical text. Basically, her curriculum units direct the teacher to find the lowest common denominator and to build from there until each pupil finds his or her level of competence. Although highly structured, this method is open-ended. "Never be afraid to change a work pattern," the manual tells staff members. "If you observe an easier and less complicated way to carry on, make the changes and they will be made in the procedure file."

Corinne's manual has nothing of the lockstep methods often evident in the teaching manuals of big-city schools. Corinne Owen's constant goal is the welfare of her students; she wouldn't dream of holding on to a method that can be improved upon. Indeed, many of the changes in her early manuals came at the suggestion of the Lambs themselves.

Her only objective was to give the Lambs something that they needed.

Her guidelines are crystal clear—free of the foghorn language often found in other procedural manuals. "Work procedures should be written for the slowest learner," she wrote, "with alterations made for the more capable people."

Corinne's approach is to outline a particular job pattern in her own mind. She then breaks the task down to its smallest possible components. Necessary equipment is listed much as one finds the ingredients in a recipe book. Then the procedure is described in a precise order—each task broken down to several components. Drawings illustrate certain procedures so that the instructors can present a familiar work layout for the developmentally disabled worker. The detailed procedures act as training manuals for the supervisors as well as the workers. The uniformity of the procedures means that new employees can be trained rapidly, and the workers do not get a mixed message.

Evaluation forms allow each supervisor to measure the worker's progress against specific criteria. In this way, more able workers can advance; the less able can be guided to simpler tasks.

Corinne has an inherent consummate patience. For some students, work intervals are as brief as five minutes. Gradually—sometimes over many months—the retarded person's ability to work on a given project improves only a little. But Corinne continues her gentle prodding until her students master the task.

In addition, she insists that allowances be made for the students to develop socially and intellectually. "That's always one of the most difficult problems to overcome," she said. "We can't have them just doing simple tasks. They've got to be allowed to talk, to enjoy." Clearly, she doesn't want to introduce the assembly-line mentality.

"Always teach from a positive point of view," she wrote. "After you have thoroughly taught a person a particular task, assume and expect him to be successful."

"Give one order at a time," she advised. "Most of our

young people cannot assimilate several orders and carry them through properly. Show them exactly how you want the job done and then gradually withdraw as the young person gains confidence. But always remember that our young people will need some kind of quiet, unhurried support all of their lives."

The core philosophy of Corinne Owen's manuals remains in place today. Today, the Vocational Training and Placement Department has elaborate procedures for job training and placement. Lambs are carefully placed in positions on the Farm and in the community. They are carefully supervised, with stopwatch efficiency but with the same patience Corinne Owen initially insisted upon. Workers may change jobs. No one is forced to do tasks for which he or she has capability but no interest. All are encouraged to find their level of competence—and then some.

Corinne has written manuals for the pet store, the Country Inn, and the gift shop. The pedagogical advice they contain could readily serve as a model for parents—or employers. A brief page on motivation, for example, states that it can be achieved through humor, love, and a feeling of being needed. Sometimes, a stern attitude is required, such as saying, "This is the way we're going to do it." But more often than not, the task gets done best when it is thoroughly salted with approval and acceptance.

The manuals' instructions illustrate Corinne's and Bob's most deeply held beliefs. They could serve as a creed for a family. Examples:

• We cannot stress enough how vitally important it is not to talk down to young people. They may lack intelligence, but they do not lack feelings.

• At the Lambs Farm, administrators, teachers, and our young people share responsibilities through love. We talk to each other as friends, and that means a regard for intelligence, no matter how slim. It means a regard for feelings.

• The merest hint of a "them and us" attitude will do more to destroy what you are trying to build than anything you can think of.

- Above all, be patient. These young people have faced lives few of us can imagine. If you do become discouraged and frustrated, just think for a moment of the discouragement and frustration they must be feeling.

- Before the day is over, always assure the young persons that you still love them, care for them, and need them. Make sure they know that you do not expect a repetition of the offensive behavior, but that tomorrow is a new day and the slate will be rubbed clean.

- Don't try to con these young people. They'll turn off in a second.

"You know," Corinne observed years later. "When you come right down to it, isn't this what we are all after?"

✦ Lambs Tales ✦
Sam Ross

The silk-screening that began at the Bonaparte School and carried over to Retarded Children's Aid was also used in the Lambs Pet Store on State Street. Because it didn't take a dozen Lambs to staff the store at all times, alternative activities were necessary.

Corinne Owen found some space in the back of the store, which served as office and storeroom. She began teaching silk-screening to the Lambs. This time, however, she intended to have them make greeting cards that could be sold at the store. It was the beginning of one of the Lambs Farm's most successful enterprises.

The Lambs could make the cards. They needed only some designs. The parents of one of the Lambs persuaded their friend, Sam Ross, to lend a hand. Sam was a retired commercial artist and the former field secretary for the Hebrew Theological Seminary. He told Bob and Corinne, "I'll do anything I can. Let me hold up your arms the way they held up Moses's arms when he got too old and weak to pray."

Sam Ross designed the first cards. Then he got involved with recreational projects. He loved to show them all the shapes he could make from a circle or a square. The Lambs learned a lot from Sam.

The Lambs had organized their own social club. They elected their own officers and planned their own projects.

Corinne and Bob were not permitted to attend their meetings, but the limited space in the store made eavesdropping easy.

One day, the Lambs invited Sam to attend their meeting. They wanted him to design a flag for the club. Sam did a beautiful design: two white lambs on a light blue background with the legend "Feed My Lambs" in red and white beneath them. The only hitch was that the flag company they contacted wanted $85 for a hand-sewn nylon flag. The Lambs Social Club had $10 in its treasury.

"Let's have a potluck supper," one Lamb said, remembering that this was how it was done in his church. "We'll invite our parents, and they can pay to come."

"But who will cook the food?" another asked.

"Dummy," Danny said. "We'll get our parents to make that, too." The retarded can be creatively manipulative.

They pulled off the supper. The parents even rented the hall. Their friend, Sam Ross, was the guest of honor.

Sam Ross worked with the Lambs until just before they moved to Libertyville. One day, his wife called to say that Sam had died. It had been his hope that he would see the Farm. The Lambs were disconsolate.

His wife worked as a volunteer secretary until the Lambs moved to the Farm. For years after his death, memorials from his friends arrived in Libertyville.

Sam was still holding up their arms.

◆ Chapter 6 ◆

State Street to Libertyville

At first, Corinne and Bob thought of finding an old brown-stone near the Lambs Pet Shop on State Street. Many of them remained in the area. They were old and run-down, but they could be renovated. Some or all of the Lambs could live in the home, and there would be additional rooms for the silk-screening, the ceramics, and whatever else might occur.

They called George Van Emden, their volunteer legal counsel. With lawyerlike thoroughness, he gave them a brief course in the legislation governing such homes. Housing anyone with mental or physical problems brings into play a vast superstructure of protective ordinances. There were fire, safety, and health precautions that translated into virtu-ally gutting an existing structure in order to accommodate a group of mentally retarded adults. After two sessions with Van Emden, they concluded that it would be far wiser to build from scratch.

They considered another pet store. In this way, they could spread the large staff around. One was available in the sub-urb of North Chicago. However, North Chicago is forty miles from the original pet store. Besides, during their long conversations as they traveled to and from the store, Corinne and Bob had concluded that the Lambs were ready for a new venture. The two were thinking of food again—a little cater-ing business or a small restaurant.

Gradually, their ideas merged. Bob began to talk of a large property. Bob and Corinne had talked often of founding a community where the Lambs could live and work together. The idea was not to remove them from society in an institutional setting. It was to provide a place for retarded adults to live, especially after their parents could no longer take care of them. Far from being isolated, however, the community would actively sell to the public.

Corinne was more skeptical than Bob. However, both agreed that they would never permit practical considerations to frighten them away from a goal. They always thought that they would fashion their dream, then look for the means.

Looking would take time, and Bob, Corinne, and the parents had very little to spare. But there was always time to talk to people who came to the store. Bob confided their dream to Julie Ann Lyman, who had written the feature article on the Lambs for the *Tribune*. Julie's husband, Lloyd Lehman, was then a schoolteacher. His job permitted him a certain amount of discretionary time. They offered him a part-time job to search for a site during the coming spring and summer months.

They were purposely vague with him, saying they just wanted a big piece of property. "We always walked into things wide open," Bob wrote years later. "We had no preconceived ideas."

The founders of the Lambs Farm have always operated on this philosophy. They have never closed windows of opportunity. Deep down, they seem to have an intuitive sense of what is appropriate and confidence that they will recognize it when they see it. That approach has aroused criticism from those who believe that each move must be planned meticulously and then adhered to regardless of experiences to the contrary. It has permitted them to be innovative. It also explains why professionals in the field were reluctant to support them.

So Bob and Corinne didn't flinch when Lloyd Lehman told them that a turkey farm was available just outside Libertyville, Illinois. As things turned out, that property was only five miles from the present Lambs Farm.

Of course, Bob and Corinne knew nothing about turkeys, but initially the notion of a turkey farm run by retarded adults seemed to have some merit. However, the owner failed to present the business of raising turkeys in an attractive way. He sickened them with his ambush approach to the sale and his gruesome course on the beheading and plucking of turkeys. Corinne and Bob tried to picture their special friends guillotining and plucking turkeys. It wouldn't be the Lambs Turkey Farm, they decided.

They searched as far away as Lake Geneva, Wisconsin—a beautiful resort area about ninety miles from Chicago. "But nothing up there spoke to us," Bob recalled. So Lloyd kept looking.

The ad was in the *Tribune*'s Sunday real estate section: "50-acre estate. Libertyville. Formerly a working farm with dairy barn and two houses. Grounds include a 15-acre lake." To hear Bob tell it, the ad leaped off the page at him.

Ideas have a way of leaping into Bob's mind and finding a home there. He then gets stubborn about them, clinging to them like a limpet. But he has a measure of common sense. Her name is Corinne.

Bob called Anderson Realty in Wheeling and asked one question: How much? Then he called Corinne and told her that the lake was stocked with fish and that the barn was the biggest in Illinois. Once fixed on a dream, reality is a mere detail to Bob Terese.

"How much?" Corinne persisted. "One hundred and eighty-six thousand dollars," he answered. "This will take a lot of prayer," she said.

Bob and Corinne, together with their new evening manager of the pet store, Ron Pierce, followed Mr. Anderson to the farm. It was a beautiful day. The ride took them past the home of their friend Adlai Stevenson, along St. Mary's Road, and past elegant farms and estates. The area was then very much in the country. It is less so now but still retains much of its pastoral charm.

Mr. Anderson crossed under the then-new Illinois Tollway on Route 176 and turned into the farm. The property was just off a busy tollway, an ideal location for a business. The lake on the property had been formed by the engineers who planned the tollway. They had taken soil to build the highway and permitted the natural springs to create the little lake. Then they had stocked it. Most likely, the owners—a man named Myron Davenport, who owned all the buildings and nine of the acres, and a man named Newburg, who owned the remaining acres—had decided to sell not long after the tollway came through.

They drove along a dirt road into the property. The barn was as big as promised: four stories with a huge silo. It had enough room to play an official game of basketball—or open the world's largest pet store.

"Used to be the Lancaster farm," Anderson said. "Their land went west of here. Too bad the tollway cut through."

He showed them the main house. It was still occupied, but no one was home. The farm was old, but the house was of a fairly recent vintage. It was the third house that had been built on the foundation.

When Corinne saw the dining room and kitchen, her imagination began to flow. She saw a small restaurant capable of seating some seventy-five people, if one included the outdoors.

They visited the second house. It was smaller—just four rooms—but would make a perfect gift shop. Corinne had been told that country inns needed something more than just a restaurant to pull in the guests. This house would be the shop.

The barn looked even bigger from the inside. It was dreary and grubby; it hadn't been used in some five years. However, the space was breathtaking—room for a pet store, offices, training facilities, conference rooms—anything they might want to do. Above the low-ceilinged main floor, there was room for at least two stories of facilities.

It was ideal—filled with faults but also with possibilities. The board of directors pointed out its shortcomings. No one runs a pet store in the country, they said. Gift shops are an awful risk, and two restaurants go broke for every one that succeeds. The worried businesspeople and parents hung crepe on every phase of the dream.

But they believed in Corinne and Bob. They believed in the capacities of their retarded children. They had spent their entire lives hearing people tell them that nothing could be done for their children. They had taken a risk with the pet store. After the discussion, when it came to taking action, they voted to go ahead.

Anderson Realty asked for some option money. The Lambs organization had only $25,000, more than enough for a ninety-day option. However, if they couldn't close in three months, they would forfeit 10 percent of the option money. The Lambs organization couldn't afford to risk $2,500.

They met with Myron Davenport, the co-owner of the property. Bob asked him if he could help out. "Hell, yes," Davenport said. "Take the option for a dollar." They called Mr. Newburg, and he agreed to go along. Bob found the dollar, but Davenport returned it to him, saying, "You're going to need every penny you can get." (After the meeting, Corinne wheedled the dollar from Bob. She intended to frame it. She took it home, put it under the linen runner on her bureau, and simply didn't get around to going to the frame shop. Two years later, Corinne's daughter, Doris, needed some money to run an errand. She found the Lambs Farm's first dollar and spent it.)

They envisioned what became the Farm as a kind of ideal community where retarded adults could live and work. It would be a place to come home to for those who were capable of working in outside jobs. It would be a retirement home—a desperately needed alternative to an institution—after the Lambs' parents were gone or were no longer able to take care of them. They had already come to realize that any retarded person who had been institutionalized for more than three years was beyond their reach.

The Lambs Farm would be a kind of shopping mall and small neighborhood. There would be twenty homes. Bob and Corinne dreamed of a fruit and vegetable stand, a gas station, a greenhouse, a nursery school, a motel—as many businesses as they could possibly operate.

Over the years, they tried a number of the projects and set them aside in favor of something else. Other ideas simply died in the telling, but experience showed that unfulfilled dreams were part of a healthy process. The alternative was not to dream at all. The alternative was institutional thinking.

For now, however, they had to shelve their dream and confront the hard reality of finding some way to finance a purchase that was nearly ten times their resources.

One parent was wealthy, but the board quickly found that he was not *that* wealthy. Early critics of the Lambs Farm program sometimes dismissed it as a facility for wealthy children. The reality is that only a small percentage of the clients have come from families with means.

Bob and Corinne approached the pet industry—they even showed slides about the Lambs before the Pet Food Institute—and suggested that a Lambs connection would be good advertising. They received a sympathetic hearing but no promise of money. The advertisers of pet products were very cautious about endorsements. Puppies do get sick. It is part of their process of growth. A few sick puppies in a cage in the window of a pet store could hurt an advertiser's image.

The turndown was fortunate. Looking back, the directors realized that product endorsements could ultimately skew the program. Some advertisers might want to run the program with a view toward marketing their product. The program would lose its integrity.

The ninety days were passing swiftly. With a week to go on the option, Bob and Corinne didn't have a single prospect to fund their purchase.

It is the stuff of which movies are made. With three days

to go, Julie Ann Lyman came into the shop with a suggestion. "Why don't you let me call Clement Stone?" she said. "You've got nothing to lose at this point."

W. Clement Stone represented a classic entrepreneurial success story. With a limited education and a salesman's irrepressible hope, he began selling insurance to middle- and lower-class people. Often called "couch policies," the coverage amounted to little more than $1,000, the premiums to only a few cents. But the buyers viewed their policies as burial insurance or something for their children. The majority outlived the life of the policy and commonly presented the paid-up policy to their children as a wedding present. The children promptly cashed the policy and bought a couch.

Stone had made a fortune selling insurance. He was just becoming known in the Chicago philanthropic community for his boundless enthusiasm, fueled by his philosophy of Positive Mental Attitude, and his generous challenge grants. He would later become even better known for his support of Republican causes and his interest in rehabilitating criminals. Coincidentally, Julie Ann Lyman had done a feature on him for the *Tribune*. Stone had told her to let him know if she heard of a worthwhile project that might pique his interest.

Julie made the call right from the shop. Without telling Stone what she had in mind, she asked to see him. Stone told her that he was preparing for a three-month trip around the world with his wife, Jessie, and that he was leaving within twenty-four hours. Hurriedly, Julie explained the situation. "I'm not going to the office tomorrow," Stone said, but he agreed to meet with Julie for ten minutes the next morning at her apartment. He said he would bring his lawyer, Russell Arrington, an influential attorney and a leader in Illinois politics.

Corinne and Bob didn't go to the meeting. They didn't know Stone, and they were too nervous even to go to the store. They took the day off. To this day, Corinne believes that, as she lounged in her backyard hammock, hoping and praying, she sensed that Stone had bought the property for them. She started to get up, and just as her feet touched the ground, the phone rang. It was Bob.

"We've got ourselves a farm," he told her.

Stone had agreed to purchase the farm. He would retain ownership, and the Lambs Farm would pay him what they were paying to rent the State Street store.

This arrangement continued for three years. By that time, the group was reasonably settled on the Farm; the businesses were progressing; they were meeting their goals. These were the kinds of results that genuinely pleased Stone, who has an unflinching bootstrap mentality.

A frantically busy man, Stone had little time to visit the Farm, but he carefully observed its progress. Corinne and Bob kept him apprised.

One Sunday morning, he appeared with Corinne and Bob and Dr. Karl Menninger on "Cabbages and Kings," a TV talk show that often focused on activities akin to the Lambs Farm. After reviewing the progress of the Farm, Stone announced, "You're doing great work. You're meeting your goals. I'm turning the deed over to you."

♦ Lambs Tales ♦
Judy and John

The late Dr. Lawrence Peter wrote a tongue-in-cheek book having to do with people reaching their level of incompetence. His basic thesis was that workers often work hard and, as a consequence of their diligence, are promoted. Eventually they reach a level beyond their competence, where they spend their lives in quiet frustration. Further, they unwittingly inflict pain upon others.

Dr. Peter's famous Peter principle applies with tragic seriousness to the dilemma of the retarded. Left in the loving but sometimes frantic care of others, they are pressed beyond their level of competence or, conversely, permitted to merely vegetate and become even more retarded. The delicate balance of avoiding both outcomes is hard to achieve.

As mentioned already, Corinne Owen discovered early that the abilities of mentally disabled individuals vary widely. The secret of good training is to help each of them find his or her level of competence. Then, by connecting them to a group of people who are of like mind and interests, efforts must be made to help them to mature within that level. This does not mean that changes to other interests cannot be made. It means simply that the retarded should be led—not shoved—to find their place within society's complex structure.

John came to the Lambs Farm when he was nineteen. He

had spent several years at a well-known school for the retarded in the East. After a brief observation by Corinne and Bob, it was obvious that all he wanted to do—all he *could* do at the time—was polish his cowboy boots and play with his coin collection.

John was frightened of everything. If someone walked near him or attempted to speak with him, he ducked and cringed as if he feared physical punishment. It wasn't just people. He feared cars and doors—and, of course, dogs and other creatures. He rarely spoke. The only time he seemed not to be frightened was when he was on the telephone. When he spoke to people in person, he mumbled. On the phone, he spoke clearly to the disembodied voices. They weren't quite real. They could not harm him.

John had virtually no energy. He could do a job. In fact, he functioned at a high level, at least when compared with other retarded. But he had no staying power.

Bob and Corinne began working with him in brief intervals. They assigned him to jobs that took only a few minutes. Gradually, they increased the "dosage" until John could work for fifteen minutes without growing weary. Slowly, they got him to the point where he could work up to two hours without a break.

As his stamina grew, his confidence increased. After two years, although he still didn't speak clearly, his work habits were as good as the other Lambs'.

Then it happened. One night, while a group was driving back from an outing at Chicago's Riverview Amusement Park, Danny said, "Wasn't that dodge 'em ride great? Banging into everyone? I really liked that."

"Me, too. I liked that ride a lot," John said. The boy who rarely spoke, except over the phone, was talking with his friends.

Corinne and Bob said nothing. It might scare him back into silence. Two years of waiting had paid off. He was with people he loved and trusted. He came out of his shell.

After that, John progressed rapidly. Within a few months, he was working at Meyer's Pet Shop in the Carson's complex. Still later, he found a full-time maintenance job at the post office. By 1965, he was earning over $500 per month.

The affluence created problems. He had purchased four watches and had become prey to at least one of his fellow workers, who "borrowed" $100 from him. Fortunately, the money was recovered.

John had come a long way, but he had reached his limits. He needed the loving protection of his family and of the Lambs Farm community.

Judy seemed to have no such fears. She was good at what she did. She loved birds and animals and went quickly from the Lambs Pet Store to outside employment at Meyer's, where her constant chatter was a contrast to John's quietness.

She worked part-time for the first year, then decided that she wanted to work full-time. Her parents agreed but were concerned that she would lose touch with the Lambs. But Judy wanted the full-time job. She had an independent streak—one that exceeded her competence.

Competence has to do with layers of ability. All people must do a balancing act involving their personal and vocational lives. Judy was still doing her job quite well, but when her mother died suddenly and her father suffered a breakdown shortly after, Judy had virtually no reserves to draw upon. Her brothers and sisters were unable to take her in, she had lost contact with the Lambs, and before long the community learned that she was living on her own.

Continuing to assert her independence, Judy refused help. In time, her dress and hygiene left much to be desired. She couldn't cook well; her diet suffered.

One of her sisters went to the Lambs Farm and asked for help. Corinne and Bob arranged to have her take care of the birds at the store and found her a room with a caring family. But she refused both offers.

"Judy willed herself over the barrier to normalcy," Bob recalled. "The result was failure. She became a very lonely woman."

The Lambs invited her to their Christmas party. She came

and behaved badly. She continuously tried to stroke Corinne's face, forcing Corinne to speak to her alone. She was desperate for the love and affection that the Lambs had offered her but could not accept it.

She had overextended herself badly. Her intellectual and emotional resources were simply not enough for her to maintain herself in a complex world. The delicate balance had been badly thrown off.

In a sense, Judy had exceeded her level of competence. In this, she was little different from the gifted individual who exceeds arbitrary emotional or intellectual boundaries and becomes the victim of stress. Some very successful people can become prisoners of their success as much as Judy. Chances are, had she remained within the Lambs Farm, she could have eventually found a level at which she could live and work without the pain of loneliness or failure.

♦ Chapter 7 ♦

On the Farm

The Lambs Farm is a charming, campuslike property with paved roads, proper signage, ample parking, and carefully groomed grounds. In 1965, however, it looked just like what it was—an abandoned farm.

"I saw nothing but a pet shop," Bob Terese recalled. "I try to avoid areas that I'm not good at."

Not only was Bob avoiding areas in which he had no competence; he and Corinne both were avoiding reality. Through a member of the board, a contractor, Bob contacted two major architectural firms about the feasibilty of turning the barn into a pet shop. The first firm recommended simply tearing the barn down. The ceiling was too low, they said. The shop would be impossible to heat. The walls were scarred with drafty cracks.

The second firm had lofty ideas. They wanted to turn the barn into a kind of a Taj Mahal for pets—an impractical, expensive showplace. Their preliminary drawings showed a two-and-one-half-story window for the east wall through which birds would be displayed. Corinne thought of the difficulty of cleaning the cages, but she and Bob were so anxious to get the job done that they felt adjustments to the plan could be made later.

Throughout the winter of 1965–1966, the architectural firm continued to delay. When the firm suggested that the

113

contractor-father on the board do the work, it became clear that they had lost interest.

The organization had lost precious time. Their cash reserve of $25,000 was dwindling. The State Street store remained open, providing employment and income, but the operation had to move to Libertyville if the dream would ever be realized. Further, there was the agreement with W. Clement Stone, which anticipated that the project would be up and running within a short time.

The property was woefully in need of work. The farm's roads were rutted. "Ducks could float in the potholes," Bob remembers, with only a little hyperbole. What are now sidewalks were simply gravel paths. (Not long after the tea room was opened, an elderly woman sought out Bob in his basement office. "Why don't you pave these paths?" she asked. "Those pebbles hurt my feet." When Bob told her that there was no money available, she asked how much it would cost. Bob pulled a figure out of his head. "About $1,800, I suppose," he said. A week later, the Lambs Farm received a check from Lillian Kelly, the owner of a rooming house on North Dearborn Parkway. She remained a close friend.)

Neither Bob nor Corinne had the faintest idea how the old barn could be turned into a pet shop. They had only a vision and friends. They returned to Myron Davenport, the barn's previous owner, for advice. He introduced them to Dave Hardyn, who had worked on the barn before it was acquired by the Lambs Farm. Hardyn was more pragmatic than the previous architects. He told them that he could put a 50′ × 50′ pet store inside the huge barn.

It became a family project. Trevor Owen, Corinne's husband, and Jim Ireland, her son-in-law, worked with Lambs' parents and the Lambs themselves to rip out the milking stalls and to level the floor. Bette and Jim Ireland lived at the farm. Bette taught music to the Lambs; Jim did many repairs. One of the Lambs' fathers found a friend who would install heating for the place. It was far from perfect, but by September 1966, the Lambs Pet Shop was in business.

From September through December, business was virtually nonexistent. "People didn't know we were in Liberty-

ville," Bob said. "Some days, we went without a single sale."
The only real income was from the State Street store. To
keep the business solvent, married staff members agreed to
work without salary. In spite of every economy, the organization came dangerously close to not being able to pay its
basic bills.

They needed some timely publicity. Bob turned again to
Stuart List of the *Chicago American* and several other people
in the media. List came through as he had earlier. He introduced Bob to columnist Herb Lyons and society editor Eleanor Page. Both gave the store booster shots in their columns.

Page put them in touch with Fay Peck, wife of insurance
executive David Bell Peck III. Fay Peck was on the brink of
success as an artist and simply did not have the time to help
the Lambs. However, she told her husband of their dilemma.
He passed the hat among his well-connected friends, including Bill Wirtz, Phil Sweet, and John McInnis. Within four
months, they had raised $12,000, enough to get the organi-
zation through the first winter. Later, Fay Peck would donate
paintings to adorn the walls of the tea room.

Eleanor Page's mention of the Lambs in her column caught
the attention of Mike Dunn, retired president of Magichef
Stove. Dunn had been a white-collar executive with a reputation for resuscitating ailing companies. But he wanted to do
manual work at the Lambs Farm. Arriving each day in his
luxurious Cadillac, Dunn worked as a carpenter in the old
barn, saving his executive talents for his work on the early
board. He worked for a full year, at least forty hours each
week, providing his own tools and building the kennels in
the barn and, later, the silk-screening room.

Even as he worked, Dunn observed the bookkeeping techniques at the pet shop and found them to be terribly inade-
quate. He set up new systems for the pet shop, the dining
room, and the gift shop, as well as systems for occasional
events such as the Flower Show and Country Fair. Later, as
a board member, Mike Dunn streamlined the entire accounting process and helped the board to make annual income
projections.

The first volunteer staff people at the Libertyville location, exclusive of the parents, came from the Moody Bible Institute's aviation program, which was held nearby. They worked in the dining room with the first Lambs, helping to cook and serve in the fifty-seat restaurant.

In the pet shop, Betsy Getz became the first "professional" employee. She came from an affluent family and initially worked as a part-time volunteer. When she asked to become a full-time volunteer, Bob declined, preferring to hire her at minimum wage. "I wanted to be able to tell her what to do," he said, "and you can't always do that with volunteers." Betsy accepted and was soon running the pet shop like the expert she became.

Although things were improving, the early efforts were filled with frustration. The pet store was still not fully under way. Sales remained slow. The Lambs now numbered twenty-four, and there wasn't enough work in the pet shop to occupy them all. In an effort to make their venture survive, Bob and Corinne decided to open a fruit and vegetable stand.

Initially, they planned to grow some corn, tomatoes, and pumpkins on the land. Using their own variety of what would come to be called "networking," they contacted the office of the Lake County farm director. They were advised to visit Matt Beemsterboer, a farmer and corn stand proprietor in nearby Grayslake. Bob took a few of the young men with him. He recalls little from the visit, but Beemsterboer was impressed by their need. He volunteered to go to Libertyville and put in their crops.

He planted some beans for them as well as tomatoes and pumpkins. "Forget the corn," he told them. "I've got more planted here than I'll need this summer. I'll give you some."

The farming venture didn't work. The staff wasn't big enough or knowledgeable enough to train the Lambs. They learned that the soil east of the Des Plaines River wasn't really good for farming. They gave up growing their own vegetables after only one growing season.

But, through some tough times, the vegetable selling proved a modest success. One of the fathers, Ted DeMata, built an attractive stand by the roadside. "It was a lovely stand," Bob recalled. "It had a blue awning on top. People were attracted to it."

Local farmers donated produce to the farm. Things were fine in daylight hours, but at night the stand proved too attractive for vandals, who smashed it to pieces one night not long after it opened.

Bob was ready to close the business down. But it was virtually the only business on the farm at the time. He decided to do what he had a genius for doing: get some publicity.

He contacted the local newspapers in Libertyville, Mundelein, Lake Forest, and Waukegan. He told them the story of the Lambs, their tiny stand, and the thoughtless vandals. The papers sent reporters and photographers to take pictures and to cover the human-interest story. Understandably, it attracted a great deal of attention. The Lambs Farm had never advertised itself as an enterprise for the benefit of the retarded. Many people learned for the first time about the work being undertaken at the Farm. Business improved dramatically.

To provide variety, the Lambs Farm began buying vegetables and fruit from the Tom Naples Fruit Market in Melrose Park. It was the largest market in the greater Chicago area, and Bob had come to know Pat and Joe Naples when he stopped to buy vegetables for his family while en route to the Farm. The brothers became increasingly generous to the Farm, selling them goods at cost and not charging cartage. In effect, Bob recalled, they ran the stand by remote control.

Eventually, Pat and Joe began donating upwards of twenty-thousand ears of corn and hawking it themselves as volunteers at the stand. Customers were told that they could take all the corn they wanted in exchange for a contribution. Pat and Joe—and eventually parents and other volunteers—would cajole the customers to be more generous. "Hey, mister," Pat would yell, "with that Caddy you're driving, you're gonna throw in one lousy buck?" Inevitably, the customers coughed up more for the Lambs.

Bob found a large cooler, a castoff from a closed flower store across the street from Chicago's Drake Hotel. It was installed in the barn and was used to hold the more fragile fruits. The cooler was but another example of the often haphazard but providential manner in which things happened to these early Lambs. Needs arose. Corinne and Bob would begin "connecting." Somehow, the needs were met. There was no long-term planning beyond the vision of where they hoped to be someday. But somehow it worked out.

Their days began to take shape. Corinne worked in the pet shop, the tea room, and the printmaking shop she had set up in the back of the barn. (Orders for their greeting cards grew so rapidly that at one point Corinne began bringing work home. "Enough!" her worried husband ordered. "You're working too hard." She worked anyway, often seven days each week, to fill the orders.) Bob was everywhere—supervising the fruit and vegetable stand, working on the barn or in the evolving dining room.

Both continued to solicit gifts by telephone. They appeared at luncheons, dinners, and lodge meetings of groups such as the local Lions, Kiwanis, and church groups. They showed slides and told stories. Then they opened the floor for questions. Sometimes one of the higher-functioning Lambs would come with them, often answering questions from the group. Support was not always immediate, but they raised awareness levels. They were planting the seed.

Gradually the restaurant took shape. At first, it opened only for private parties. In 1967, it opened for Sunday brunch as the Lambs Shepherd Inn. The first cooks were Corinne, who made the biscuits, and wives of the Moody Bible students.

The first meals were simple fare—chicken à la king was a favorite. But the ingredients were all best quality. The chicken was all white meat, and the biscuits were homemade and generous. They were the kind of meals one expected in a country inn. There were several serving areas, each designed so that the Lambs could do the serving.

They attracted women's clubs, garden clubs, church

groups—friendly, captive audiences. Bob and Corinne would welcome the group, then tell them the story of the Lambs. After helping to serve the meal, a few of the Lambs would entertain the group with songs. "It was a perfect match. The groups loved it," Bob remembered.

The Minarik family entered the picture just as the Lambs Farm was considering opening for Sunday dinner. Fran Minarik was the owner of Golden Harvest Catering. She had heard about the Lambs through a friend who had a mentally handicapped daughter. When she met Bob and Corinne, she became involved immediately.

It turned into a family project—Fran Minarik, with her husband, Anthony, and their three daughters, Sharon, Bonnie, and Carol. The Minariks made it possible for the Farm to open on Sundays—and later Saturdays—to the general public. Fran was the professional and the idea person. She brought equipment from her business and eventually turned the tea room into a restaurant. The menu expanded to include baked ham, pot roast, and old-fashioned stew. The serving was buffet style, and the portions were generous. Corinne had carefully broken down the tasks so that the Lambs could staff virtually every aspect of the service. The Lambs served, poured coffee, brought desserts, and cleared tables. Most important, they mingled with the customers, chatting with them, sweeping away barriers, building confidence in themselves and in the public. (Bonnie Minarik, now married to Herb Schneiderwind and pursuing a career in banking, recalls her initial problems mastering the art of dishing up ice cream. "Don't worry," one of the Lambs told her. "We'll learn you.")

Soon the fifty-seat dining room was crowded every weekend. At $3.95, the family meal was one of the best bargains in the area. Families sat on the porch of the home-restaurant, waiting their turn and chatting with the Lambs.

"I wasn't that interested in my own business," Fran Minarik recalled years later. "I lived for the weekends when I could work with people whom I loved."

The Minariks were involved in the first Country Fair. It

attracted over ten thousand people, far beyond expectations. Before long, they ran out of food. Fran sent her family to their home and had them clean out virtually every usable item. "Soon we were serving just biscuits and gravy," she said. "But the crowd didn't mind. There was such a wonderful spirit about those fairs." It is a spirit that remains to this day.

Fran Minarik and her family helped to train other volunteers. Many were spouses of Trinity College ministry students. Having worked at a camp for years, Fran understood large-group catering. She was able to keep costs down, and with so much donated food and labor, the Country Inn was a success.

Fran persuaded her husband, an engineer with ADA Metal Products, to do much of the electrical work in the inn's kitchen and dining rooms. Tony soon became as involved as the rest of the family. He has been a member of the board for over twenty-five years.

In 1968, Sharon Minarik, now a schoolteacher, became the founder of the Lambs' bakery. With Doris Owen Servey, Corinne's daughter, she went to Pennsylvania Dutch country to observe the Amish people and their simple baking methods. It was there that they learned how to make jams and jellies. Soon after, using a recipe created by one of the Lambs' mothers, the bakery introduced its famous butter cookies.

The Lambs Country Inn is now a full-service restaurant. Just inside the entrance to the property, it continues to attract customers for luncheon and dinner and to do a substantial banquet business. It also prepares the meals for the forty residents at the Intermediate Care Facility.

Thirty-five percent of the Lambs employed on the Farm are involved in food-service work. Food service manager Judy Close, an employee since 1980, describes the operation as primarily a "vocational training center." Now the State of Illinois sends clients to the Country Inn for training in restaurant service.

In the restaurant business, where high turnover is a fact of life, Close's professional staff has averaged eight years of service. The reason can be traced to the Lambs themselves. "We're almost a family," Close said. "We have an added responsibility, and that puts us in a kind of sister-brother relationship."

Operating the restaurant may be the hardest work that the Lambs do. It requires a good memory and good judgment. Most of the employees are higher-functioning retardees; most work well under pressure. But, as with all the Lambs' activities, the primary emphasis is always on the training of the Lambs themselves. In Close's words, "This translates into 60 percent training and 40 percent actually doing the job."

The Country Inn has never been a money-maker. But it manages to break even, and it does a significant repeat business. It may have lost some of the intimacy of its earlier days, but it remains a beacon for the other Lambs Farm ventures. Because it is more like other restaurants, it can better serve as a training center for Lambs who will be working in competitive employment. Just as important, the Inn is the place where the public can meet members of the Lambs Farm community. They are no longer secluded in their homes or hidden in institutions. Their service at the inn means they will no longer spend fruitless years and empty lives.

◆ Interlude ◆
Ruth Wilkomer

"Parents should be expected to do some work for the Lambs. I know they don't require it, but I really think they should do something, if only to buy a few tickets. I think it's an obligation."

Ruth Wilkomer is now elderly and infirm. Struck by a car in 1987, she has undergone five operations and still requires a cane to get around. But she continues to do volunteer work for her beloved Lambs. She has been a member of the board of directors since its inception in 1961. As such, she is the longest sitting board member on a board known for its long-term loyalties.

Ruth and Harry Wilkomer's son, Danny, was one of the twelve original Lambs. The Wilkomers met Corinne Owen and Bob Terese at Hull House. Danny had been introduced to Hull House through an uncle who had seen an ad in the local paper for a sheltered workshop. Bob and Corinne didn't teach Danny but got to observe him and to know him. They came to know Ruth and Harry through Danny.

When the Lambs were being formed, the Wilkomers met at Delilah White's apartment to discuss the future of the proposed pet store. "There were only about a dozen of us," Ruth recalled. "Some stayed. Some didn't. We liked it. Danny liked it. So we stayed."

The early meetings were held at the local YMCA and, later,

at the Playboy Building on Walton Street. Ruth's initial involvement was with the women's board, which met on the same night as the board itself. "One night, the board found that it needed a secretary," she recalled, "so I was named to the board of directors and have served since."

The Wilkomers' experience at the Lambs Pet Store on State Street was filled with nostalgia, warmth, and laughter. Danny, perhaps the highest functioning Lamb of the group, was among the first to be given a key to the store. He opened the store in the morning, sometimes worked the register, and performed high-skilled tasks around the store. Harry Wilkomer, a tool and die maker, spent weekends helping to install shelving and counter space, teaching Danny to wire the display cases.

"We didn't live far from the store," Ruth recalled. "A few times, the police called us, and Danny had to go down to rescue a racoon that was caught in the washroom and to help catch a monkey that was on the loose in the store. It was a lot of fun."

The operation was simpler then. Parents and their young adult children sometimes gathered at the conference table in the back of the store and made cat-scratching poles. Harry would bring wooden posts from work; another Lamb's parent, who worked at Goldblatt's department store, got the management to donate carpet remnants. The Lambs fashioned the scratching posts and sold them in the store at a significant profit. The materials, after all, had been donated. "They were good posts," Ruth recalled. "*Popular Mechanics* did a how-to article on them."

Danny Wilkomer left the State Street store as part of its first experiment with outside employment. He has worked in another pet store, a bank, and at Carson Pirie Scott department store. He worked for a time with the Lambs in Libertyville but returned home, where he is now a valued helpmate to his mother.

Ruth Wilkomer has been the chair of the annual Christmas party since its inception. She shared the task with her husband until his death. She has been aided by Gertrude and

Joe Small and Carl and Marjorie Collmer. Another couple serves as "angels" to the project, picking up the tab for all of the Lambs' tickets.

The Christmas party is primarily a celebration for the Lambs themselves, the employees, parents, and friends. It has been held at a succession of restaurants and hotels in the greater Chicago area, all of which offer their facilities at reduced rates. The party now draws over five hundred people each year.

Ruth Wilkomer has seen great changes during her nearly thirty-year association with the board. Today, a forty-member board works with a staff of twenty-seven professionals, including a full-time volunteer coordinator. Nearly two hundred individuals and groups now volunteer more than twenty-five hours each year to the Lambs. The figure does not include over fifty individuals and corporations who contribute valuable services and materials.

Janet Jesse has been a full-time, staff-level volunteer coordinator for the Lambs since 1986. Before that, Virginia Denton, wife of board member David W. Denton, had been virtually a full-time volunteer coordinator for five years, working without compensation "Thanks to Ginny, I came into a well-established, well-managed operation," Jesse said. "It was not a broken-down mess. I could expand on it."

Volunteers now come from every segment of society. Board custom dictates that at least one-third of its members be parents of the Lambs. Initially, most of the volunteers were women who were primarily homemakers. Today, according to Janet Jesse's office, many are young professionals of both sexes "who are discovering that life isn't just a quest for money."

The volunteers help in an astonishing variety of ways. There is the pleasantly mundane: peddling hot dogs at a special event. But other volunteers use their professional skills to help individual Lambs. Accountants prepare their tax returns; hairdressers teach them grooming; teachers at the skill school teach Lambs the basics of a computer; seminarians from the nearby University of St. Mary of the Lake, a major Roman Catholic seminary, work one-on-one with individual Lambs. Students from the Dr. Scholl College of Podiatric Medicine do foot examinations; Cecil Reimers conducts blood testing. Some elderly, retired people work virtually full-time in the bakery or gift shop. Members of a Presbyterian church group called the Fifth Wheel Club drive the Lambs to church on Sundays. The EWES of Lake Forest have been helping in the skill school for years; the Lambs Helpers, under the direction of Ruth Pompian, provide myriad services. Celebrities such as the legendary Mike Ditka, head coach of the Chicago Bears, serve by attending events such as the Good Shepherd Award Dinner. (In a celebrity-oriented society, someone of Ditka's status can command $10,000 for simply showing up.)

The combined efforts of the parent volunteers represent what fund-raisers term a "living endowment." Translated into lay terms, it means that the Lambs Farm would need millions of additional dollars to compensate for the services generously contributed by the parents.

The volunteer involvement began when Bob and Corinne started making a few phone calls to parents of potential Lambs. The early meetings were held at the Playboy Building because the room was free. But it was hardly a corporate boardroom. The first women's board, in fact, met in a room that had to be reached by passing through the women's rest room.

The volunteers are people in the spirit of Ruth Wilkomer, who still attends board meetings and still speaks forcefully of the Lambs Farm's future.

"We need to build up the businesses even more. We need to get more of our wares in other stores. We could do it. It's a wonderful board, and that Gerald Friedman [executive director] is very well thought of. He knows his business."

Ruth Wilkomer continues to energize volunteers whom she has never met but who are attracted to the Lambs. They catch the same spirit.

◆ Chapter 8 ◆

A Grain of Mustard Seed Becomes a Tree

Mary Kowalik became a part-time volunteer worker for the Lambs Farm in 1970. She had heard about the organization through her brother and sister-in-law, Karol and Audrey Orawiec, who had managed the pet shop since 1968. She started in the Country Inn one or two days each week. By this time, the Lambs had the pet shop, the vegetable stand, the inn, a tiny gift shop, and the beginnings of a bakery business.

The operation was still largely run by trial and error—"management by walking around," as one expert now describes such a method. But it was working. Bob and Corinne continued to find people like Mary Kowalik who had something to give. The Lambs did the rest.

Gradually, Mary began to spend more and more time at the Lambs Farm. Her twenty-year career there parallels its remarkable expansion into a complex of small businesses. After volunteer work at the inn, she took full-time employment at what she termed "the farmers' market." It was actually the beginnings of what was to become Aunt Mary's Country Store and Country Kitchens, which she now manages. The farmer's market was located in an old tool shed. Now renovated and expanded, it serves as the Women's Board Thrift Shop.

"At first we just sold fruits and vegetables," Kowalik

recalled, "but eventually we got a refrigerator and started to sell cheeses and all sorts of things, including candy."

The concept of acquiring items for resale started from the day the Lambs Pet Store opened on State Street. With the exception of the greeting cards, virtually every product—including the pets themselves—was acquired through outright gift or wholesale sources. In time, the Lambs would produce their bakery goods, jellies, and hand-dipped chocolates. Today, the Lambs Country Gifts Catalog lists over thirty-five gift items, not including the greeting cards. Their inventory is largely sausage-and-cheese baskets, gourmet nuts and chocolates, together with the Lambs' own preserves, barbecue and chili sauces, and bakery goods.

From a casual, drop-in, almost bucolic business, it has grown into a slick, well-oiled operation. Individuals and corporations can order through a toll-free or fax number and charge their orders on a variety of charge cards. Today, 40 percent of the store's business is through the catalog. Aunt Mary's Country Store is a charming, beautifully appointed store that compares favorably with any commercial enterprise of its type. In addition, the Lambs do private production and packaging for three companies, largely supplying salsas and Bloody Mary mixes as well as the Lambs' preserves under a private label. Their own labels are now carried in a number of franchise and chain stores.

"The Lambs must be involved in everything we do here," Kowalik said. "We buy our candy in bulk so that they can box or bag it. Much of our prepackaged goods come unlabeled so that they can learn to put on labels. Our employees, who have been with us a long time, are trained to train. We're not simply a store."

Things do not always go smoothly. Lambs are trained for upwards of six months for some tasks. But mistakes are made. Quantities can get mixed up, and labels can end up on the wrong jars. Occasionally jar lids are slightly askew, and the product gets moldy. But corporate customers are very understanding. They are aware of the purpose of the program, and they are patient. Chances are, their error rate is no higher than that of their competitors.

The Lambs' candies followed the establishment of the bakery. Initially, the staff tried a do-it-yourself approach, poring over books and manuals in an attempt to understand the art of candy making. Nothing seemed to work.

Finally, a Lambs-connected physician encouraged a patient who worked for a large local candy company to come to the Farm and teach them. The man taught them how to make peanut brittle. The brittle was good, but the Lambs wanted to do chocolates. They found an old-world chocolate maker who had a shop in Wilmette. He came twice each week for six months, teaching the trainers and the Lambs. Soon, the Lambs' hand-dipped chocolates became another staple. Later, the Department of Rehabilitation Services of the State of Illinois supplied them with four candy-making machines, and the operation expanded.

Mary Kowalik runs the Country Store like a mother superior. The store is open seven days each week, and the Lambs are scheduled for a five-day work week. They are evaluated, tested, and counseled, and their wages are set. Lambs enjoy all fringe benefits, including paid vacations and holidays. "To most, salary increases are a motivation," she said. "To others, it just doesn't matter. They're just like the rest of us."

Over the years, Lambs employees learned a great deal from each other. Bob Terese was the idea man and problem solver. Corinne had the ability to break things down into learnable units. Their personalities and their techniques filtered down. While the Country Store has enlarged considerably, the chemistry of the shop remains the same. "If it changes," Mary Kowalik said, "they might as well just put a shopping mall here."

The essential difference in all the Lambs organization's enterprises is that their primary mission is to educate and train the developmentally disabled, not to generate profits. "We never worried about making money," Bob Terese said, "so we didn't plan for success. We just looked for things that our people could do, and we went ahead."

Like many long-time employees, Mary Kowalik had had no experience with the retarded. Her first helpers, Danny Tucker and Dennis DeMata, were the first retarded adults she had ever met. "At first, I was so fearful," she recalled. "I was afraid to turn my back. I was actually afraid they were going to hurt me physically. It took time to really come to know them. I didn't know how wonderfully honest they are, how they don't know how to lie and how I had to learn to take them as they are because they will say exactly what they know. I had to learn how to treat them."

Today, twenty-one Lambs work with four paid staff in the Country Store and production center, which makes the jams and candies. "We still do everything with our clients in mind," Kowalik said. "We don't purchase anything or bring in new machinery without them in mind."

The philosophy of the Lambs Farm is most apparent in the Country Store and silk-screen shop, where virtually all tasks are performed in the open. Kowalik is typical of Lambs-centered employees who have learned how to pace themselves and their retarded colleagues. She speaks of six-month orientation periods, emphasizing that the first task is to get to know the worker and then to apply a mix of directive training and endless patience.

"They can learn, but they get confused," she said. A lot of the confusion appears to stem from anxiety. Once the anxiety level is reduced, learning takes place faster.

Today's Country Store is so well established that it's difficult to find trace marks of the days when, in Kowalik's words, "We didn't know about the next paycheck, and we hesitated to spend fifty dollars for fruit."

The silk-screen business that dates to the Bonaparte School and Hull House has now evolved into the Persimmon Tree Card and Gift Shop. It employs some fifteen Lambs and has been so successful that it has occasionally had to contract a portion of its orders to keep up with the demand. From the very start, according to Corinne Owen, they have worked to ensure that the cards were of the best quality and competitive with cards produced by commercial houses. Sales are helped by large orders received from corporations and from the sale of silk-screened aprons, T-shirts, and sweatshirts for businesses, teams, and other organizations.

More important, the silk-screening operation permits the

employment of moderately functioning retarded adults who may not have the skills required for the Country Inn or the pet shop. Still using concepts developed by Corinne over two decades earlier, the production tasks have been broken down so that the less gifted members of the community can learn.

In 1969, the year that saw the opening of the Country Store, the Lambs Farm opened a children's farmyard and a petting zoo. These have remained popular attractions. Visiting children can get close to the farm animals and ride the small ponies, all cared for by the Lambs.

In 1981, the women's board established a thrift shop in the old tool shed, which had served as a farmers' market and gift shop in earlier days. Basically a resale shop, it has been a profit center from its inception. "It can't miss," one observer said. "All the items are donated, and all the help is voluntary." In 1989, the shop was enlarged. The effort has made the women's board one of the distinguished donors to the community, with cumulative contributions of over $250,000.

A year later, the pet shop was completely renovated and made measurably more attractive. Today the pet shop sells purebred and mixed-breed dogs—a change from its early days, when mixed breeds were the norm. Further, only 10 percent of the community—perhaps fifteen Lambs—are involved in animal care. But the massive barn continues to be a beacon for the property. The picturesque barn is now used as one of two Lambs Farm logos.

In 1985, the Country Kitchens—an expansion of the bakery and confectionary operations—opened and doubled the production of the Lambs' most popular food items.

In 1986, Sweet Street Ice Cream Parlour opened in one of the recycled farmhouses. It attracts a great many children, especially in the summer. According to manager Amy Gahart, "Some of the children back away. They're tentative. But then they adjust to the presence of the retarded." The experience may help them to avoid the more pervasive fears of their parents.

The Sweet Street shop employs only two Lambs, but

David and Paul are so outgoing that they give the place its warm and friendly spirit. During busy summer months, the shop employs high school girls to do some of the clerking. Gahart says that the sometimes immature teenagers need to be brought to task for lateness or other infractions. But they will beg to stay if they are threatened with dismissal, because of their fondness for the Lambs.

Gahart herself, one of the youngest on the staff, exemplifies the Lambs-centered employee. Such people have difficulty thinking about working elsewhere or even being away from the property for a long period. They have all the usual employee concerns and are not free from the typical job frustrations. But the hold the Lambs have on them is pervasive. "They are my brothers and sisters," Gahart says. "I couldn't work anywhere else. I just love Paul and David."

In 1981, the new Country Inn was dedicated. Former First Lady Betty Ford came to the dedication and cut the ribbon. She also served as hostess for the guests. Mrs. Ford is one of many distinguished guests to visit the Libertyville property. The Lambs have played host to entertainer Carol Burnett, U.S. Senators Alan J. Dixon and Paul Simon, advice columnist Ann Landers, former Senators Charles H. Percy and Adlai E. Stevenson, TV personality Lee Philip, and Illinois governor James R. Thompson—all of whom have been designated honorary board members.

In 1989, the Lambs Farm's latest business venture, a miniature golf course, opened. It was built with the help of eighteen corporations and foundations, each of which had agreed to sponsor a golf hole. Sponsors included Abbott Laboratories, Allstate, Arthur Andersen & Co., Chicago and Northwestern Corp., Chicago Tribune, Hollister Inc., Illinois Bell, Jewel/Osco Stores, John F. Kennedy Health Care Foundation, John Morton Co., Kemper Group, McDonald's Corp., The Popcorn Factory, the Fred B. Snite Foundation, Stein and Co., and Walgreens.

According to Jack Stein, longtime board member and president of the board that approved the golf course, "The Lambs facility is a kind of public park. We attract 300,000 visitors each year. The golf course is a natural for us."

In 1981, the Lambs Sheltered Workshop opened. Now located less than two miles away, it employs some forty members of the community, who do mailing, packaging, and simple assembly work. For Bob Terese, the workshop program represents a change in thinking. "We founded the Lambs to get away from some of this kind of work," he said. "But now it's OK. The operation has changed. Now there's a place for the sheltered workshop."

Part of the reason for a change of heart has been the vastly increased sophistication of the training and supervision. Professional vocational training and placement staffers ensure intensive training and a wide variety of options for the Lambs. Within the newly acquired large building, a work center manager works with four trainers, who make certain that the jobs are not simply busywork.

While a number of the contracts are ongoing, staffers solicit within the community to find new contracts. In 1988, for example, staff found sixty-two new contract jobs for the shelter. Participants can change tasks simply by asking and qualifying. Kris Hasemann, manager of the center, says that the training of the clients has improved considerably. "They're good workers. Absenteeism is very low, and they socialize very well."

Lambs work shorter hours at the shelter. The workday begins at 8:45 A.M. and ends at 2:30 P.M. The early departure permits the Lambs to attend classes in a skills component program aimed at improving their daily living skills. Back at the Farm, workers also have an opportunity to take part in exercise programs.

Today, 146 Lambs are working in one or more of the Lambs Farm businesses. They are part of a work force that is responsible for 42 percent of the organization's income. In the process, the Lambs themselves earn modest wages. Their earnings support them.

As a consequence, they relieve the State of Illinois of a tremendous financial burden. Had these retarded adults been declared wards of the state, the annual cost for taking care of each one of them would be in excess of $30,000. Instead, they are wage-earning, taxpaying members of society, supplying a large portion of their own needs. Although it initially viewed the Lambs Farm as a crackpot operation, the State of Illinois now sends some of its clients there for job training.

In 1979, the Lambs Community Placement Program was formally established. It had its roots in the outside employment that some of the original Lambs found while still at the State Street store. Outside placement dates to 1964 but was formalized some fifteen years later. Today, Lambs working away from the Farm are involved in retail, clerical, childcare, maintenance, and laundry work.

Outside employment has been successful because staff follow up on their placements for no less than six months. Trainers first learn the job, then teach the new employee. Employers appreciate the intensive pre- and post-placement training, because it reduces turnover. In 1989, every trainee was successfully placed.

Lambs like working away from their residences on the property, but most are happy to return to the comfort of the community. The community continues to experiment with independent living. A Waukegan residence was opened in 1980.

A new trend, called "normalization" by the professional community, has had some support from the professionals at the Lambs Farm and from the Lambs themselves. However, the administration is moving cautiously. Prejudice against the retarded remains a serious issue. Neighborhoods that might accept a home for the developmentally disabled are often areas where retarded adults would be instant victims.

However, the prospect of increased "off-campus" living and working continues to be a lively topic. Independent living arrangements for those with the greatest competence would relieve crowding at the Farm and create room for new residents. The waiting list for prospective participants is now around 100, necessitating a five-year wait for some applicants.

Ideas for new ventures continue to surface. Currently, the

organization is looking for a donor to supply them with pasta-making equipment. Pasta would be an ideal base for the Lambs' savory salsas. The idea of a greenhouse-nursery—one of the original suggestions—continues to interest some members of the community. The success of the Christmas business has prompted some to suggest a year-round Christmas shop, and some still feel that a day-care center is feasible. With the success of the bakery, candy, and gift shops, it has been suggested that the Lambs Farm open outlet stores in suburban shopping malls.

Whatever the case, Bob Terese said quietly, "We will always continue to look for things that go on inside people. We'll never put profit ahead of people, and we'll never try to be a production line at Ford Motor Co. I'd much rather work for the circus."

"He's Improving—
I Can Tell"

His immaculately tailored suit marked him as a successful executive. He walked with the confidence normally associated with men who enter paneled boardrooms and take their place at the head of the table. It's been called "corporate cool."

"My time is severely limited," he told the volunteer coordinator at the Lambs Farm. "I can only give you a few hours at a time, and I think that I could best be used in administration or fund-raising."

It was an intriguing facade. Mike Scully (a pseudonym) was not the usual Lambs Farm volunteer. He was doing time the soft way. The court had found him guilty of one of those ubiquitous white-collar crimes. Scully had been sentenced to several hundred hours of community service, and the judge had assigned him to the Lambs Farm to complete his court-appointed hours.

Scully's ego was in shambles. It was held together by the dried glue of past successes. Used to giving orders, he played mind games with himself in the hope of masking his crime.

He didn't fool anyone. The court's papers were on the volunteer coordinator's desk.

She gave him room. There was no need to destroy his ego completely. His shame was just under the white shirt. Let the convicted criminal do his time with dignity.

137

There wasn't anything for Mike Scully in fund-raising. He probably would not have been good at it. She assigned him to work directly with one of the Lambs. Scully might be able to teach him something—how to make change, understand something about taxes, work a simple computer.

Scully would do his time and get out of there. He wasn't pleased with his first assignment. Retarded adults are often high on energy and low on learning. But he stopped short of asking for another. He complained, but he knew he was a crook. If his papers went back to the judge, he could be required to do time at one of those white-collar prisons.

"I don't like it," he told the coordinator when he got his time cards signed. "He's too slow. But I'll stay with this kid. He's probably as good as you've got."

They worked together—Scully and the retarded young man. The Lamb knew nothing of Scully's background. He saw him as a friend—someone he could talk with, someone who could answer questions. There is a very good chance that the mentally handicapped man could sense Scully's own insecurity and loneliness.

"I think he's enjoying it," Scully told the coordinator months later. "He seems to be learning something. He's improving—I can tell."

Months passed, Scully doing time, the young man "learning something." Somehow, Scully's voice was softening. The edge was off it. But no one asked. There are a few "volunteers" doing court-appointed time at the Lambs Farm. Some are working off DUI (driving under the influence) offenses. Others, like Scully, do longer time. There is too much to do at the Lambs. There is no time for the luxury of questioning court-directed volunteers.

One week, Mike Scully couldn't get to the office to submit his time sheet. So, the volunteer coordinator called his home to complete the necessary paperwork. She reached his wife.

"He's a changed man," Scully's wife said. "He's just not the same."

◆ Chapter 9 ◆

Living at the Lambs Farm

"This is Mayberry, U.S.A.," one long-term employee said of the community at the Farm. She was exaggerating, but there is a kind of bucolic, ambling pace about the neighborhood that is infectious. One only has to make eye contact, and one will be greeted. Just as important, the visitor will be remembered.

It may be that an indefinable mood change visitors experience on entering the Lambs Farm property causes them to invest the residents with qualities they do not really possess. However, it does appear that Lambs remember the people they have met. Perhaps it is because their minds are uncluttered by social considerations that block out much human interaction. Whatever the case, there is a touch of television's Mayberry.

In 1980, nine group homes were constructed along the perimeter of the lake on the Farm. The founders and administration did not intend that all the homes would be built at once, but this was one of the terms of the $2.6 million, forty-year loan from the U.S. Department of Housing and Urban Development. In that same year, the Waukegan House was opened—the first "off-campus" facility, now home to four residents capable of a higher level of independence. It was also the year that the Country Inn was completed and Betty Ford came to cut the ribbon.

The homes are classic form-follows-function architecture, designed to provide a safe and uncomplicated living environment. Fire doors, doors to common areas, bathroom doors, and doors to the twelve private bedrooms, six bathrooms, and the overnight supervisor's apartment give the houses a mazelike feeling. Oversized exit signs and emergency lighting fixtures reduce the homelike atmosphere somewhat, but overall the homes are little different from those in any suburban development. Common-area furnishings, donated largely by parents, add to the atmosphere.

The dozen bedrooms give the homes their character. Six men live downstairs and six women upstairs in all but one of the homes, where the upstairs-downstairs arrangement is reversed to accommodate three female residents who have cerebral palsy.

Each resident's room is equipped with a bed, bureau, and chair. For the rest, the Lambs are permitted—in fact, encouraged—to decorate their rooms "within reason." The decors are triumphs of imagination and individualism. The small rooms are carefully cluttered, largely with additional furniture, TV and stereo sets, wall cabinets, and family bric-a-brac brought from home. ("They get on us if we don't keep them neat," said one resident who spoke facetiously off the record.) Walls are decorated with art, family pictures, and a bewildering variety of posters, most of them of sports figures. The Chicago Bears, perhaps the most famous football team in the world, and the Chicago Bulls, with Michael Jordan, the most famous basketball player in the world, are prominent not only in the men's bedrooms but in a number of the women's as well. (Chicago Bears coach Mike Ditka is a Lambs Farm icon. He has visited the Farm, been a speaker at their Good Shepherd Award Dinner, and, more important, had his picture taken with many individual Lambs.)

Lambs hang their own artwork in their rooms. Libby Creigh, a Lamb since 1969, is an accomplished watercolorist who hopes someday to sell her works at one of the craft shows. Another Lamb has the ceiling of his room virtually covered with beautifully rendered model planes.

The policy of giving the residents wide latitude in decorating their rooms helps them to express their individuality. It also reduces the institutional atmosphere.

The varying decors are no accident. They are simply another expression of the Lambs Farm's mission and spirit. Residents are encouraged to be individuals; institutional uniformity is quietly discouraged. Rooms are not numbered; there are names on each bedroom door; residents have individual keys to the house and to their own rooms.

Conversations with residents reveal that they continue to press for even more individuality. Conversations with staff reveal that such rugged individualism is slowed only by the practical considerations governing time, money, transportation, and the like. "I'd like to go shopping alone," one Lamb said. "You know, just take a bus and come back when I felt like it." Lambs now shop for groceries and personal items at local shopping centers. However, because transportation is always a consideration, they travel together.

Approximately 150 Lambs live on the property. Forty are in the "dorm." Completed in 1976, it houses residents needing closer supervision of their personal and medical needs. Called the Intermediate Care Facility, it cares for the more developmentally disabled, who would have difficulty in an independent living situation.

The nine on-campus group homes, called SLAs (Supportive Living Arrangements), accommodate residents capable of semi-independence. About thirty-five of the SLA residents commute in one of the ubiquitous vans to outside jobs at schools, hospitals, and corporations.

House managers coordinate the complex schedules of the residents. It is a high-burnout, high-turnover job requiring the efficiency of an office manager and clergylike patience. "They leave because the paperwork gets to them," one long-time Lamb observed. A resident manager agreed. Each form has a purpose—indeed is necessary. "I want this paperwork," she said. "It's necessary. We must record their expenditures. Their parents have to know where the money is going. But it does take an awful lot of time." It is like being stoned to death with popcorn.

The Lambs themselves complain mildly that they are over-protected, but they are not anxious to see dramatic change. The alleged overprotection adds up to a degree of emotional comfort. The house customs are emotional pegs that supply a certain stability. When the Lambs complain, it is not without a certain saving humor. "They even do our taxes for us," Michael said, "and you can't beat the price." (In 1989, Michael earned $18,000 at his outside job. Before he came to the Lambs Farm, his only employment had been as a country club caddy. Among the Lambs, unemployment is nonexistent. They are not a burden on the community. More than likely, once the walls of ignorance are completely eliminated, candidates for public office will attempt to visit the property in search of their vote.)

The first van carrying the Lambs to work in outside employment leaves at 5:00 A.M. Most Lambs work basic 8:30 A.M. to 5:00 P.M. jobs and return to their homes around 5:30 P.M., looking as weary as any other worker. Those who work on the property have somewhat shorter hours and can participate in additional learning and recreational activities.

Meals are prepared twice each day on workdays and three times on weekends. Watching the Lambs preparing their own meals in the kitchen with the help of the resident manager is reminiscent of the days when Bob and Corinne first attempted to teach their charges how to cook at the Bonaparte School and at Hull House. A few Lambs, now in their mid-forties, can recall their days at the State Street store. Five of the original twelve Lambs are still at the Farm.

Everyone takes a turn at cooking. Budgeted to just under $400 weekly per house for their food, the Lambs shop at local supermarkets, help to plan menus, work in pairs to prepare meals, and share the cleanup. There is a certain amount of regimentation, necessitated by the fact that the Lambs and their resident managers devour a total of about 225 meals each week in each house. However, they carry the tasks off with a certain low-key casualness. Then they join hands and say a brief grace. ("One of the former resident managers taught us this grace. We've been saying it ever since.")

The food is plain but healthy. Fruits, salads and vegetables are served in abundance. Even relatively harmless coffee is rarely served; the Lambs prefer fruit juices and milk. Liquor is not served, and smoking is virtually nonexistent. The Lambs do not live in a social vacuum. They are well aware of the risks of smoking. ("I used to smoke," David said. "It nearly ruined my voice." But another chimed, "I'm going to California for my vacation this year, and I'm going to have a beer." Then he laughed and went his way.)

When the budget permits, a house will go out to dinner, generally at a franchised, mid-range restaurant where a dozen adults can eat for under $75. It isn't easy, but they manage, largely because they are very sensitive to budget needs.

Health and exercise are constant topics among the Lambs. Many suffer from one or more physical disabilities. Most are on some form of medication. The experience has made them medically sophisticated. In recent years, there has been a stronger emphasis on proper diet, exercise, and weight control. The Lambs are weighed regularly, and the obese are counseled to eat less and exercise more.

The basement of the Intermediate Care Facility contains an abundance of exercise equipment. The Lambs Farm Recreation and Leisure Services Department has created programs that assist participants in becoming aware of how exercise, along with a sensible diet, can increase good health.

There is a strong emphasis on "lifetime" sports—ones that participants can continue to enjoy even as they become older. The program involves everything from aerobics through golf. Lambs can swim at a local high school, and, weather permitting, there is a wide variety of track and field opportunities. The new Founders' Building, begun in late 1989 and named in honor of Bob Terese and Corinne Owen, will add even more athletic and other leisure-time facilities.

The Special Olympics competition is only a small part of the Lambs' recreational program. It is conceptually akin to the Olympics themselves, although it has many events designed exclusively for the mentally and physically handicapped. It adheres to the older tradition of the Olympics that taking part is more important than winning. The Lambs hold the Special Olympics in high regard. In virtually every room, the medals they have won are prominently displayed. The Special Olympics has gone international, and a number of Lambs have traveled to regional meets and won gold medals.

"Life here is almost too busy," one Lamb said. "We look forward to Sunday, when things slow down a bit." Those who wish to attend church services are transported to the church of their choice on Sunday. The educational and athletic events are optional. Lambs who wish to can simply go to their room after dinner and watch TV, although, as one Lamb observed, "They'd come after you to get you involved in something."

Turnover at the supportive living homes is very low. Many Lambs have been in the same houses since they were completed in 1980. As a consequence, they have formed close ties. In 1990, House Three, for example, had not had a new resident in over a year, and the young man who moved in then had been living in another home on the property for four years. As a consequence, the residents of each home become like families.

The success of the residential program has caused its own set of problems. Some families contact the Lambs Farm administrative offices in the belief that their family member can be accepted immediately. "One of our problems is that grieving families frequently call us, informing of a death in the family and the need to place the retarded family member," said Jackie Cohen, director of residential services and training. "They simply don't understand the demand. It makes it very hard on them—and us."

It is difficult to avoid stereotyping the members of the Lambs Farm community. By definition, they are moderate-to high-functioning adults, many with similar physical problems. It is easy, then, to invest them with other shared characteristics—even virtues—that simply do not survive closer scrutiny. Clearly, they are a close community. Everyone can readily recite five or more facts about another resident. ("Oh, she lives in House Two. She works at Allstate and has been here since 1981.")

Many Lambs appear to be veritable storage units of personal and community history, with precise information as to their arrival dates and significant events at the Farm. ("I started at the Lambs on February 2, 1969," Libby recalled. "I was one of the first three residents when they dedicated the dorm on March 12, 1976.")

A developmentally disabled person's memory is most likely no better than any other person's. Perhaps because their minds are less cluttered with other information they can retain images and information that are important to them. While some are gifted with recall, the others may simply remember because the dates were important plateaus in their lives. ("I had no friends," Michelle recalled. "Here, I have lots of them.") Such experiences can sharpen memories. Longtime staff members simply shrug at such observations. Their most common analysis: "Look, they're just people. They're people with special problems. Some have skills we can't explain. Nothing more."

A popular movie, *Rain Man*, in which Dustin Hoffman accurately portrayed a gifted but severely autistic adult, implied that mentally handicapped people have compensating gifts, such as incredible memories and computerlike math skills. In fact, the syndrome Hoffman portrayed is rare among autistic people. At the Lambs Farm, a few are capable of a certain math wizardry, and one can play the piano without the aid of sheet music. But the remainder are simply limited or gifted within very normal ranges.

Another stereotype perdures. Lambs appear to be younger than their years. A forty-four-year-old woman will look at least ten years younger. ("I'm always being called a teenager," one said. "I'm thirty-one.") The answer may simply be that most Lambs do not affect current dress styles, often preferring the casual dress of younger people. More likely, their apparent youthfulness stems from good diet and exercise, proper medical care, abstinence from smoking and drinking, and a relatively stress-free environment. Again, the experienced staff only shrug. Such stereotypes are luxuries that may contain the harmful seeds of patronization.

J. Curtis Jones, president of the Lambs board from 1988 to 1990, believes that the inherent gentleness of the Lambs carries over to others and clearly accounts for the atmosphere at the Farm. Lambs have few hidden agendas. They are not afraid to discuss their mental and physical limitations. Their conversations are remarkably free of tension and, with company at least, are marked by great deference to one another. Members frequently point out the accomplishments of another member. Conversations are often marked by polite exchanges such as "excuse me" or "I'm sorry I interrupted." Good manners seem to be the oil that keeps the machinery of close living working smoothly.

Conversations are marked by gentle humor at someone's expense. Jokes may have something to do with one's weight or height or talkativeness, but they are made totally without judgment or the cutting edge of moral rebuke. The Lambs do not view physical or mental shortcomings as moral offenses. Kidding is followed by loud laughter and genuine expressions of caring. The word *love* occurs far more often than in so-called "normal" social situations.

Further, for a group of adults whose average age is just under thirty-five, the Lambs exhibit a great degree of physical contact. Such contacts are remarkably free of the sexual tension often associated with displays of affection such as hand-holding and back massaging. It is not completely accurate to say that retarded adults retain the simplicity of children. More likely, they simply do not have some of the emotional baggage of others.

Emotional flare-ups appear to be settled quickly. ("Now, don't give me a hard time, David," the house manager said. "I've had an awful day. Get off my back!" Minutes later, David was chatting amiably with her and observing over his shoulder, "We love her.") Again, there is a risk of stereotyping, but viewing the interaction, it is difficult to escape the conclusion that retarded adults living in the social climate at the Lambs Farm have difficulty bearing grudges or nursing emotional wounds. They appear to be emotionally healthy people.

Virtually all have suffered serious illnesses in their lifetime and remain on some form of medication. They exchange information on the nature of their medication as well as a great deal of sympathy for each other's physical problems. ("Boy, the first time Amy had a seizure, I was really scared," Steve said. "But she taught me what to do.")

The large dining room and the scheduled meals ensure that the "family" eats together—an increasingly rare practice in noninstitutional settings. They do not appear to tire of one another's repeated stories, although they are quick to react when someone exaggerates a real or imagined happening.

Living together for years, they have a special vocabulary composed of slang and shorthand for the various departments on the grounds and outside. Clearly, the community has developed a language of its own that may now extend to several hundred words. While this is not uncommon in any close-knit community, it is simply another example of the "normalcy" of handicapped people. "They're just like us," Bob Terese said with an occasional touch of impatience. "It's really very simple. They are simply ordinary people with special problems. We're all the same. It's simply that we have different levels of understanding."

Over dinner at the Country Inn and in conversations after dinner at one of the group homes, some longtime Lambs Farm residents spoke about their lives and their ambitions for the future of the community.

"Independent living with minimal backup support should be the option for numerous Lambs [Farm] residents," Libby Creigh said.

Libby is president of the Residents' Council and one of its most articulate members. Paradoxically, Libby's love for her community is exceeded only by her desire to move away. She has met with the community and developed criteria for independent living. She dreams of a townhouse or condominium that would serve as a home to Lambs capable of taking their own medication, free of behavior problems, and able to hold a position in the community and to use its transportation system.

The call of some Lambs for independent living is simply another expression of the Lambs Farm's mission. From the day that Bob Terese stepped off his bus and entered the world of the retarded, he—and later Corinne—would attempt to gently push the Lambs to greater personal achievement. Although professional has replaced personal leadership, the thrust remains the same: Give them roots, then give them wings.

Michelle Hendrickson is treasurer of the Residents' Council. She came to the Lambs Farm in 1980 and worked in the bakery. But in recent years, she has been a clerk at Baxter Travenol, where, she said, "I am treated like anybody else, and it feels good."

Michelle is one of three residents in House Three afflicted with cerebral palsy. Like Libby, she views the House Three as her home. She wants to join Libby in independent living so that "the public can see and learn how far we have come and that we can be successful at what we do, just like anyone else."

"In the long run," Michelle added, "we can feel better about ourselves by taking care of ourselves, by paying our bills, and by living independently."

Michael Kurschner now works at Fort Sheridan. His salary has increased 61 percent since he started there just a few years ago. He has lived with severe epilepsy since childhood but remains optimistic that the doctor "will get the medication right." He must take thirty-two pills each day to control his seizures. Michael may be the most verbal at House Three. He, too, supports the move to even more independent living but speaks for the others when he says that he wants to remain attached to the central Lambs' community.

David Sundheim is irrepressible. He works at the Sweet Street shop and is in charge of safety at the residences. He wants to remain on the property for a few more years, then share independent living for a few more before getting married.

His dream of marriage represents another growth out of the successful program. While friendships are never discouraged, the organization's current policy is that no married couples may live on the property. Marriage presents a bewildering variety of complex problems, but the administration is reluctant to tell people what to do. Since their days at the State Street store, the Lambs have had only two marriages. One has endured over twenty years; the second lasted only two years. Few Lambs talk seriously of marriage. One said simply, "I have enough to do just taking care of myself. I've already got enough on my plate." Yet it is remarkable to note that no member of the community will be simply told no. Lambs are respected, not cared for.

Lambs speak openly and proudly about their progress. They do so with none of the cant associated with comparable conversations among high-functioning adults. They have a sense of the dignity of labor. Someone who works in the kitchen at the Country Inn is praised as much as one who goes to work in the corporate community.

Steve hawks jams and jellies at the Country Store. At forty, he has been a Lamb since 1968 and still has ambitions. "I can work a typewriter," he said. "I think I'll talk to the voc [vocational] counselor." Most likely he will someday, but his ambition will be tempered by the close friends he has made at the store. Lambs have the gift of putting personal considerations over ambition.

Marsha completed fifteen years at the Lambs Farm in May 1990. She works at Wire City, the sheltered workshop, doing contract work. "I want to stay here," she said. "Why leave? I love it here."

The sentiments of Libby and Marsha define the delicate balance that the board and administration must achieve in plotting the future of the community. Not every Lamb is ready or willing to live in an often indifferent and competitive world. Proponents of "normalization" or "mainstreaming" may be well intentioned, but according to experienced staffers at the Lambs, many developmentally disabled residents would find the pressures of the world outside the Lambs' community to be inordinately stressful.

The present living situation may indeed give some Lambs a false sense of security. Further, community prejudices remain strong. In late 1989, a Chicago suburb had to be compelled by the court to permit a group of retarded adults to establish a group home. The presenting objection was that the neighborhood was not zoned for such an "institution." Other housing opportunities for retarded adults are often in areas with social problems that would strain even the most resilient city dweller. Staffers are reluctant to sound overprotective or patronizing, but independent living in some areas would present more problems than it was meant to solve.

The organization will tread carefully into the future. Their first steps will be to complete the administrative and learning center. Then, with one Lamb already sixty-five and several others in their early sixties, planning for a retirement facility will be initiated. Somewhere along that path, they will establish some carefully planned independent living. They are anxious to do so. It will open places for more Lambs at the Farm.

The very fact that a retirement home is being planned is a tribute to the improved condition of the nation's retarded population, especially those who have benefited from the attentive care at the Lambs Farm. One uncle of a resident, commenting on the celebration of his niece's thirty-ninth birthday, recalled that the physicians had told her family that she would most likely not survive her teens. The life expectancy of most retardees is about fifty-five, but the number continues to climb faster than for the population at large. The Lambs Farm is planning for a life span that will see the residents into ripe old age.

Steve started in 1968. "My parents are wonderful," he said. "But I was very sheltered. I went to a good high school, but the program for people like us was out of the Middle Ages. Here, I can find living space for myself."

Patti Horgan is the "baby" at the Lambs. She was only sixteen when she entered the program on State Street in 1961. Bob Terese drove her each day from Itasca, Illinois, a distant suburb. Today, Patti Horgan is a valued employee of the Grove School, a special school for handicapped children. Still mildly handicapped herself, she now cares for and educates others.

The Lambs Farm philosophy has come full circle.

♦ Lambs Tales ♦
Libby

When Dr. Karl Menninger was a student at Harvard Medical School, he came under the influence of Dr. Elmer Ernest Southard, a man Menninger described as "far ahead of his time in many ways." Southard brought psychological treatment out of institutions and into daily life. At a time when mental retardation (or deficiency) was regarded as an unalterable state, not subject to treatment, Southard believed not only that people with this condition could be helped, but that so-called "normal" people could learn much from them.

Libby Creigh is not a "typical" Lamb. There really are no typical Lambs. Each can tell a story, much of it tinged with loneliness, pain, and frustration. However, Libby can articulate her experiences and thus speak for her family at the Lambs Farm. Further, the Lambs Farm's administration guards the privacy of the residents. Access to them is only with permission. Their personal files are carefully protected.

Libby has spoken before. Her life can be told from existing Lambs Farm publications, local and national media, an interview on ABC's "20/20," and her own touching letters. Libby has been showcased often. In 1976, she was chosen to give Betty Ford a tour of the Lambs Farm during the first of her two visits to Libertyville. She visited Illinois governor Richard Ogilvie during his term in office.

The administration is not anxious to single out any one

participant. It is simply that, at forty-two, Libby has been a Lamb for just over half her life and, in many other ways, represents a composite. Her fellow Lambs take pride in her exposure. She is their elected president. She embodies the Lambs' spirit. Besides, Lambs take pride in each other's accomplishments. It's their way.

Libby was born with cerebral palsy. It affected one side of her body. Her right hand can perform only simple tasks. Her weak right leg causes her to limp. In addition, until 1979, when she was in her early thirties, she suffered from unexpected severe convulsions, not unlike epileptic seizures. In 1967 and in 1979, she underwent brain surgery. Following the second operation, her seizures ended. She has not had to take medication since March 3, 1982, a pivotal day in her life, which she recalls with glee.

Libby graduated from Sunset Ridge Elementary School in Winnetka, Illinois, in 1962, the same year her father, John, died. She was one of 1,170 graduates of New Trier High School in 1966. For one rather unhappy year, she studied at Lincoln Junior College. She attempted to major in art, but her seizures were getting worse, and she was away from her family and friends. She tried college in part because her elementary school principal had predicted that Libby would not make it past the fourth grade. She wanted to prove something to herself—and the principal.

Elementary school was tough. In a 1975 interview with Ruth Moss of the *Chicago Tribune*, Libby recalled that children threw sand in her face, beat her to the swings, blocked the slides, and stopped the merry-go-round so that she couldn't play. Little kids can be terribly cruel, partly because of subliminal fears implanted in them by parents who say, "Don't play with her; she's retarded [crippled, etc.]."

Like most Lambs, Libby was blessed with a loving family, but the early years were marked by loneliness and cruelty. Her seizures were frequent and disturbing to her care givers.

High school was much better. Some teachers took a special interest in Libby. She came to like English and history. Libby has a remarkable memory for historical trivia. During her early years at the Lambs Farm, while working in the Country Store she often engaged visitors by testing them on their American history. In the process, she provided many of them with an opportunity to speak directly with a developmentally handicapped person. Fears dropped away.

Following the year at Lincoln and her first surgery, she became a volunteer at the Hadley School for the Blind. But her mother, Beverly Creigh, recalled that it hadn't been enough. "She had no social life. She had to keep busy. That's part of her makeup."

As soon as Libby recovered from her first surgery, she came to the Lambs Farm. She heard about the Farm from a friend of her mother's whose backyard Libby used to walk through en route to school. The first years were as a commuter. She worked in the silk-screen shop, the bakery, gift shop, and dining room. When the first residence was completed, she moved in.

"I can do some things others can't do," Libby said. In a statement filled with wisdom, she said, "We balance out our weaknesses."

"Libby cannot be part of the normal world," her mother told Patricia Fleming in an interview for the *National Observer*, "but she comes painfully close. For so long, there was no real place for her. She had her volunteer work, but that wasn't enough. She had no social life. I hate to even think of what her life would be like if it weren't for the Lambs. She's found her world."

Libby spoke of her seizures with a frankness that dispelled any discomfort in discussing them. "I had to wear a brace when I was a child," she said. "I had a lot of leg therapy, and that made my leg better. But I have cerebral palsy, and you just don't outgrow cerebral palsy." Her condition also has given her a wondrous sensitivity to the handicaps of others. "In a way we are handicapped, but in a way we're not," she said. "We've got a lot more on the ball than most people who think they do. I may be prejudiced, but it's hard to understand someone else until you have to go through the same thing or something similar."

If there is a genius to the Lambs' community, it is in their emphasis on understanding others and on making friends. Their patience is extraordinary. It is not life in slow motion, simply a pace that accepts all limitations. At the Lambs Farm, no one has to look like anyone else. There is no effort to make "them" look like "us." The Lambs are not taught meaningless information simply so that they can appear to be like "normal" people. But they are encouraged to acquire the basic tools of living and to explore what interests them, whether it be art or outdoor cooking.

Libby chose art. She does cross-stitching and macramé, but it is her watercolors and occasional pencil portraits that reveal her talent and her gentle nature. "I used to sketch my friends when we were traveling on the train and, later, when I lived in the dorm," she said. She has hundreds of watercolors, all competent, some extraordinary. She dreams of having her own booth at the annual crafts fair.

After some fifteen years working at the Farm, Libby earned a job at Allstate. "I loved my jobs at the Lambs," she wrote, "but I wanted to see how far I could go." At Allstate, one of the cooperating employers with the Lambs Farm, Libby now works with two filing systems, operates a computer, and handles correspondence with beneficiaries. She earns a good salary, puts money in a pension plan, enjoys other fringe benefits, and pays taxes. Far from being a burden to society, she is an asset.

About living with her fellow Lambs, Libby observed, "Most of the time we're all friends. We can get along. Even if they drive me bananas, and some of them do, we can get along. We can set an example for an outside world that is all fighting and wars.

"Being friends, all of us can hope to show the world that there is another way, a better way," she continued. "There's much the world has to learn, you know."

◆ Chapter 10 ◆

Feeding the Lambs

The basement of one of the original homes at the Libertyville farm served as Bob and Corrine's office for many years. (They now work on the upper floor of the same building but will move to the Founders' Building when it is completed in late 1990.) The basement barely had room for the four desks that were pushed together in a quadrangle, reminiscent of the old partners' desks of the Victorian era. There was a community bathroom there, too, used by all the Lambs. It was hardly a plush arrangement, but it would remain this way for years while Bob and Corinne spent contributed funds on other priorities.

Their present offices, and those of the administration, remain modest. There is still a strong feeling that administrative costs must be kept in line as long as the needs of the retarded are unmet. The Lambs Farm spends only nine cents to raise each contributed dollar—a remarkable record when compared with other charitable efforts that spend nearly half their revenue on administrative expenses.

Somewhere in the piles of paper on their basement desks, Bob and Corinne had a notebook in which they kept a record of contributors. It was a pretty thin record. For the first few years, the organization did not even enjoy tax-exempt status. Thus, donors gave freely with no hope of a tax deduction.

In those years, most of the donations were "gifts in kind." The pet food and pet supply industry contributed pet food and supplies. There was used furniture, store equipment, recycled things that the staff begged or borrowed. The gifts-in-kind principle continues to this day. The property is dotted with donated articles—everything from electrical equipment to fire engines.

"We used to beg," Bob said. "We used to tell the suppliers that we didn't expect them to give us things free, but if they could give us things at cost, we'd pay for them. Well, often they would agree to it and end up donating the first orders."

Neither Bob nor Corinne found the calls easy. Corinne's voice is so soft that it sometimes got lost across an executive's desk. Bob has never quite lost his speech impediment. In elementary school, his stutter was so serious that he dreaded being called on in class. Years later, he was still substituting words that he stumbled on with those he could pronounce. ("A great way to build your vocabulary.") Gradually, he gained confidence. He never became a polished speaker, but as invitations to appear on radio shows such as the "Jack Eigan Show" and Don McNeil's famous "Breakfast Club" came, and when Bob and Corinne appeared on ABC, CBS, NBC, and local TV outlets, his proficiency increased.

For the first few years, the second most common form of charity was contributed services. Members of Bob's and Corinne's families, parents, friends, business associates, "walk-ons," and the like contributed a bewildering variety of talents to the Lambs. In fiscal 1989, some sixty-two individuals and firms contributed a potpourri of services and supplies—space in Lake Forest's Church of the Holy Spirit for skill classes, building products, legal and accounting services to individual Lambs, free blood tests, coaching services, and more.

Bob and Corinne knew nothing about fund-raising when they founded the Lambs. Both had good public relations and entrepreneurial instincts and, more important, a deep faith in what they were doing. Unwittingly, they understood that successful fund-raising comes not in asking for money but in presenting opportunities. For many would-be givers, their appeal was irresistible. "We never worried about whether or not the donor would give," Bob said. "We weren't professional fund-raisers who might lose our jobs if we didn't get the gift. Besides, we trusted that the good Lord would supply our needs. It wasn't in our hands."

Years later, Bob would be told, "Don't ever tell that to a professional fund-raiser!" He hasn't, but he believes it to this day.

Early fund-raising efforts followed a simple pattern: needs were identified, then Corinne, Bob, and the parents would go to corporations, foundations, and individuals and simply ask. They were received politely but, more often than not, were turned away. "We always got introduced to the second vice president in charge of seeing to it that we didn't get to see the first vice president," Bob recalled, "but our genius was our faith. We were dumb enough to believe that God answers prayer."

Gradually, some corporate gifts began to trickle in. Bob and Corinne brought home $1,000 gifts from J. C. Penney, Sears, Peoples Gas, and Illinois Bell. Gifts from recognized companies such as these served as a seal of approval for other corporate gifts.

Initially, contacts with pastors of the many churches in the area proved disappointing. "Once we invited 146 pastors for a free lunch," Bob remembered, "and only two responded. I guess they had their own needs. Besides, we weren't evangelical enough, and we were ecumenical before that became the way to go. We were mingling with Jews, and that wasn't kosher years ago. We were naive."

In time, the churches came around. They weren't opposed—just cautious about how they would distribute their parishioners' tithes. Today, busloads of church members come to have lunch at the Lambs Farm and to shop in its stores.

Progress was slow. Professional fund-raisers will confirm that, until a project is a success, people will find reasons not to give. They are cautious about giving their hard-earned money. It would take years before many donors jumped on the bandwagon.

During the State Street days, parents held modest fund-raising events—dinners and the like. Gifts came in from fraternal organizations that Bob and Corinne had addressed. Later, at the Farm, Bob produced what he termed "hokey things"—high school bands, double-decker bus rides, ice carvings, visiting chefs who would cook rounds of beef or fish, bake sales from gourmet bakeries, country and western singers, bluegrass music, magic shows—anything to make a buck.

Professionals would have shuddered at the haphazard operation. Indeed, Bob and Corinne's methods drew low-wave criticism for the first two decades of the venture. "They were viewed as gunslingers," one former Lambs Farm president commented. "It was said that they underpaid their help and that they exploited the young retarded adults who were in the program."

Employees were underpaid, but many were as emotionally engaged in the project as the founders. They accepted the low wages. Bob and Corinne were earning comparably poor salaries. Further, their philosophy and their approaches to the treatment of the retarded were regarded as simplistic. Bob still accepts the criticism. "It *is* simple!" he said with some impatience. "They only need love and respect. It's the way to work with anybody." He added, "But for everyone our philosophy offended, we had ten who would agree with us."

In spite of extremely limited resources, they steadfastly refused to raise their monthly fees for training, transportation, and food. Nor would they have separate, higher fees for the more affluent. Initial fees were only $15 per month, later raised to $25. During this period, other facilities were charging, or billing the state, upwards of ten times this amount. Even when state aid was introduced, the Lambs Farm refused to bill the state for more than they were charging independent clients, something that irritated other institutions who feared that the Lambs Farm's lower fees would provoke inquiries.

State-supported workshops actually benefited from high failure rates, because retarded adults who did not succeed in the workplace could be returned for retraining, resulting in additional fees. Private facilities, charging upwards of $25,000 per year, resented the Lambs Farm's lower fees. Residents of these homes were given excellent custodial care, but at those rates the notion that they were supposed to *work* was simply unthinkable.

Bob and Corinne's absence of a professional approach kept them focused on their primary aim: the care and education of retarded adults. They operated instinctively, drawing many of their ideas from the expressed needs of their special people. "We didn't care what the other places were doing," Bob said. "We didn't ask the state for permission to do things. There were no laws governing care of the handicapped in those early days. So we just went ahead and did it."

"We did try to go to other places to gather ideas, but they didn't resonate with ours," Bob added. "So we went our own way."

"It was hard," Corinne said. "We would go to these professional meetings. People would see us and turn away. It hurt."

Things changed only a little during the early days in Libertyville. Although people continued to donate services and goods, money was always a problem. Not long after the Libertyville property was acquired, a delightfully eccentric neighbor drove a few of her cows on to the Lambs Farm and presented them as a gift. She would later become a close friend of the community, contributing its third major gift— nearly $100,000.

The early fund-raising efforts were clearly focused. They were based on an immediate need. It was as if a given immediate need fueled Corinne and Bob's fund-raising energies.

Corinne recalled that her experience in selling reading programs and subscriptions to *Life* magazine helped her to "make the sale."

"We believed that society would be generous to any group that was making a sincere effort to help themselves," Bob said. "We always believed that if people saw that effort, they would give. I think we were able to reach inside people. I think that helped."

There were many rejections, perhaps four out of five. During one fund-raising visit to Florida, they were not even offered hospitality. With virtually no money, Bob found a room for Corinne, and he slept in the car.

Some gifts were fueled by faith and happenstance. Margaret Kehoe of the Carl Roehri Trust for Charity visited the property, asked some direct questions, and learned that the Lambs needed a mundane gift: a machine shop. She provided the money. Today, the shop is the toolbox for a complex operation, maintaining the many vans that transport the Lambs.

When William and Holly Grainger of the Grainger Foundation visited the property, they found that construction had stopped on the "dorm," the first residence. Officials had literally placed an ABANDONED BUILDING tag on the incomplete building. The Lambs had simply run out of money. When the Graingers asked why no hammers were working, Bob told them of their financial situation. The Graingers learned that it would take $246,000 more to complete the building. They gave $200,000 of the needed funds, and construction resumed.

The *Lambs Tales*, now a slick quarterly newsletter distributed to thousands, appeared not long after the move to Libertyville. It was published only twice a year and was written by volunteer professional journalists. It was mailed to anyone who had made a contribution or signed the guest book in the restaurant. The *Tales* prompted additional contributions and spread the Lambs Farm gospel.

Much fund-raising at the Lambs Farm has been events-oriented. The idea was to provide events in which the Lambs themselves could participate. The events-driven custom started in 1961, when the Lambs held their first Christmas gala, now called the annual holiday party. The first one was held at Chicago's Como Inn. The party has been relocated a number of times, partly because restaurant and hotel caterers offer generous discounts.

Over the years, single and perennial events have been added. The Lambs Tennis Ball realized $12,000 during its first year. The 1989 version netted $93,000. The women's board gala cleared a record-breaking $135,000 in the same year. In addition, the annual charity golf outing realized another $30,000.

The lake on the Lambs property has been put to good use since 1965 as the site of a professional waterskiing tournament, now considered part of the "Triple Crown" of waterskiing in the tristate region of Wisconsin, Illinois, and Indiana. There are other boat races—including bathtub and model boat races—arts and crafts shows, collectibles auctions, restored-auto shows, bluegrass festivals, dog shows, square dances, Oktoberfest and Halloween festivals.

On-property events are handled by the Operations Department with public relations backup from the Development Office. While the events do raise some money, their primary purposes are to provide recreational opportunities for the Lambs and to bring people on the property and into the Lambs Farm businesses.

In 1967, when the Lambs Shepherd Inn and the gift shop opened, Mary Lou Kogan, who was doing public relations work for the Lambs Farm, donated three months of her salary—about $1,200—so that the Farm could buy gifts for the shop. She also became the Lambs Farm's first official development officer without portfolio.

In September 1974, Bob and Corinne, together with Lew Kranz, who then served as executive director, hired Marjorie Kaiz Offer to be the first director of philanthropy and communication. "Bob called me," she recalled later. "I visited those offices in the basement of the gift shop. They told me that they had virtually no money to pay me, but I have always been attracted to the not-for-profit sector, and these were exceptional people."

Offer arrived at an interesting time. The administration of the Lambs Farm was going through a difficult transition. As she recalled it, "There was a power struggle about the singularity of purpose among the Lambs. I suppose we were moving from an intuitive approach to management to one closer to a corporate context."

"I showcased Bob and Corinne in my fund-raising efforts," Offer said. "They deserved it. There is no defense against kindness."

"They had a little group of fund-raisers working with them," Offer recalled. "Most were very kind people. The approach was very genteel and old-fashioned. Because the board ran the show, the board was placed above me, and that made it difficult from time to time. Parents of retarded children can suffer from some guilt, anger, and frustration—not all in each person, but a little in each. It made for a very delicate relationship. You needed their confidence, but you couldn't read it as friendship. It was a challenge."

Offer developed a marketing plan for each segment of the giving population. With their intuition, Bob and Corinne proved apt pupils. "They knew how to present a menu of opportunities. They had street sense," she recalled. In 1977, they raised $492,000. By 1979, the figure reached over $500,000.

Judy Marshall Jobbitt, now an assistant vice president for development at Northwestern University, joined the effort in 1977 as an assistant to Marjorie Offer.

"It was a kind of never-never land," Judy recalled. "We were a family. But there were harsh realities. We often wondered if we could fill the homes that were being built and that were completed in 1980. We wondered if the government would continue the funding. Bob and Corinne had a strong faith. They didn't ask others to share that faith, but they set the spirit for humanitarian values, and that affected us all."

During the 1970s and 1980s, the Lambs developed a

nationwide reputation. Bob and Corinne were asked to speak
to parents' groups all over the country and, as already mentioned, to serve on the President's Committee on the Handicapped. According to a highly favorable 1971 article in *Look*
magazine, they became "celebrities in Illinois social-work
circles."

By 1972, an article in the *Chicago Tribune Magazine* re-
ported that visitors in the field of retardation had come from
forty different countries to observe the work being done at
the Lambs Farm. The exposure did not produce elusive
national corporate and foundation gifts, but it did brighten
the light of the Lambs at the local level.

The vast majority of the gifts to the Lambs Farm come
from the greater Chicago area, where the organization is best
known. However, with 80 percent of all foundation money
in the area going to only 10 percent of institutions, the board
and administration have to solicit each gift personally. Parents and families already provide nearly 12 percent of the
income. "As with any volunteer-driven group," one observer
said, "some of the names in the programs are just wallpaper,
but those on the donor list represent real giving—some of it
genuinely sacrificial giving."

Francine Friedman is now the director of development and
public affairs at the Lambs Farm. A former teacher, she
worked for a child welfare organization before coming to
Libertyville. In 1989, she and her two-member staff provided the professional backup that realized over $1 million
in cash gifts alone.

Foundations, corporations, and individuals account for 27
percent of the total income to the Lambs. "We do fairly well
with corporations, a little bit better with foundations, but
the overwhelming majority of the money, perhaps as high as
70 percent, comes from individuals," she said.

"I think the fact that people are coming to realize that
mental retardation may affect them in a very personal way
makes them want to give to the Lambs," Friedman said.
"Mental retardation affects one in ten families. I'll bet there
are six million in the country. A person doesn't have to be

born mentally retarded. It can be the result of an illness or an accident."

Friedman uses her accumulated knowledge about retardation to good effect. "When you approach people and get them to realize how these things happen, then the interest level automatically rises. Then you can take it a step further and say, 'But look what a mentally retarded person can do.' Then you can go even further and say: 'Did you know that all our men and women earned a total of over $500,000 last year? And that they paid over $105,000 in taxes last year?' When I stand up before a Kiwanis group or other such groups and tell them that, they don't believe it."

"I guess we were too dumb to know better," Bob Terese said of the fund-raising efforts over the years. "We never knew any hot contacts. We weren't like those charming fund-raisers who never miss a beat. We still aren't. We often met with sincere opposition. When we bought this farm, there was a lot of board opposition. We had almost nothing in the bank. In truth, they were right. But we saw all this through the eyes of faith. The essence of faith is looking past the problem to what you want to accomplish."

The solicitation continues. Significant gifts continue to come in. Francine Friedman and her staff continue to look to the future and to new funding sources. "Nine percent of our people are over fifty now," Friedman said. "I've just written a proposal for a possible horticultural program here—one that our retired people could do. It wouldn't just be a hobby. We could use these plants on the property and in the stores. It may take another ten years, but we're thinking of it."

✦ Interlude ✦

Parents

Marie and Norman Bate are retired now. Norman owned the Bate Lumber Company, headquartered in New York with branch offices in the Carolinas and Oregon. They are several steps further up the economic ladder than the parents of most Lambs. Their affluence has permitted them to afford the best care for their daughter, Pamela, who is a victim of aphasia, a loss of the ability to understand and express ideas, resulting from brain damage. Economic considerations aside, they share the same emotional chemistry as virtually every parent.

"Everything came late with Pamela," the Bates said. "About the time a child is supposed to say 'Mommy' or 'Daddy,' Pamela wasn't saying anything at all."

In the late 1940s, the Bates moved to Jersey City in order to be near a facility that worked with developmentally disabled children. Later they found a school in Pennsylvania, where Pamela lived for five years. "It was a nice place. But it was more custodial care than learning. It wasn't for Pamela. We knew that she could learn some things. She wasn't learning anything there."

Then they heard about a place in Wichita, Kansas. "It was a disaster for Pamela," they said. She learned nothing, made no advancement.

The Bates' search for the best facility for their daughter is classic parental behavior. The Bates were able to search the country; they relocated at least five times. Other parents search their neighborhoods and cities. The search often starts with the local schools, which can be woefully inconsistent in setting their priorities—often spending more on advanced-placement courses for a tiny segment of elite students but protesting that they cannot budget funds for the mentally handicapped children of other taxpaying parents.

For years, schools provided nothing at all. Gradually, largely as a result of parental pressures, some special education was introduced at the elementary and, later, high school level. But, in the late 1950s, when Bob Terese was hired as a bus driver at the Bonaparte School, the struggling parents at that school were still virtually on their own.

Eventually, Pamela's parents found a place in Houston, Texas. There Pamela received some training as a teacher's aide. But the place was simply too big to offer the personal attention that handicapped people require for growth. Pamela's position amounted to little more than making orange juice. Her parents weren't certain of her ability to accomplish more, but they knew that somehow she could do better.

In 1975, the Bates heard about the Lambs Farm. The property was still largely undeveloped; it was only the barn, two houses, and some unpaved pathways. However, the Bates found the community "a joy to behold."

"We go back forty-four years," Marie Bate said. "We remember some of the silly stuff they gave to the retarded. What the Lambs have is a good idea and a heart of gold."

The Lambs Farm program is not a magic elixir for everyone. Today, applicants are carefully evaluated medically and psychologically. An educational, vocational, and residential history is taken, together with much other pertinent information. Applicants must apply for admission to both the residential and the vocational program. Even with such professional care and safeguards in place, not every applicant finds a home. Turnover is about 10 percent; some leave for family considerations, but others simply because the placement didn't work out.

For the Bates, however, the Farm has worked for Pamela. "She's improving each year," Norman said. "We just leave it alone. She loves it there."

Pamela works in the bakery. "She really has few problems except speech," her parents said. The Bates have moved to nearby Lake Forest in order to be near her. Pamela commutes to the Farm but will someday live there. Although she cannot communicate verbally, she understands a great deal and clearly flourishes in the companionship.

Pamela is tentative. It took a long while for her to accept the affection so often expressed at the Lambs Farm. "She liked Bob," Corinne recalled. "But she was slow to accept me. Gradually, as she saw me putting my arm around others, she let me do that with her. It's hard to teach love."

Pamela's link with the Lambs is so strong that she is reluctant to join her parents in Florida for winter vacations. She loves her bakery job. "She's being trained to do things," her father said. "She's finding common sense and a love of life."

Not long ago, Pamela taught a neighboring child to walk. Her communication skills continue to improve. "It's like playing charades," her mother said. "But we understand her."

Bob described the parental dilemma: "Quite often, there are misguided good intentions. Many parents are overprotective of their retarded children through guilt at having given them birth. 'I'll look after them,' they say. 'I'll keep them safe'—with the result that the child is never given the chance to develop at all.

"In the best home situations, the retarded children are always allowed and encouraged to do what they can do— under their own steam, in their own way, no matter how long it takes them. Asked to wash the dishes, a retarded child will complain that the water's too hot or the dishes too heavy. Finally, it's easier for the mother just to do the job herself. Besides, she runs the risk of alienating the other children if she gives too much attention to the one with special needs. Overprotectiveness, impatience, and the press of other responsibilities are all natural impediments to the successful raising of a retarded child.''

Parental pride can also interfere with acceptance of a retarded child. ''Their pride gets jammed,'' one observer said. ''They just can't accept it. It's a reflection on them.''

Once parents accept the reality of retardation without rejecting the child, he or she can more easily improve. Then, in the case of the Lambs' parents, they must let go so that their child can become part of a community where, as Norman Bate said, ''They can be puffed up, not put down.'' After a while, parental fears turn to pride. At the Lambs Farm, at least one-third of the board members are parents of retarded. Many other parents are involved in one or more of a large number of activities that fuel the Farm's energies.

Accepting the fact that one's child has a developmental handicap removes much of the self-pity and dries the tears. For Bob Terese, who can get angry at tears and pity, an appearance on Jim and Tammy Bakker's television show in the mid-1980s nearly brought him to the point of exploding. Already uncomfortable with the lavish accommodations and the royal court atmosphere of the ''Jim and Tammy Show,'' Bob and Corinne had to endure Tammy Faye Bakker's simpering questions—all of them aimed at garnering false sympathy for the retarded and their families. ''The retarded are not to be pitied,'' Bob said later. ''They should be congratulated.''

Bob and his wife took a rare vacation cruise on the famous *QE II*. The huge ship is a maze of corridors. Bob soon became hopelessly lost. Characteristic of a man who could never tolerate a restraining bit in his mouth, Bob did not even recall his room number.

The Bates accompanied the Tereses on the cruise. When Pamela recognized that the Lambs Farm's co-founder was lost, she took him by the arm and led him ''nearly a mile'' through endless corridors and hatch doors to his stateroom.

''You see,'' Bob said, ''when Lambs are involved in 'normal' society, they only make it more 'normal.' ''

◆ Chapter 11 ◆

Transition

The steps toward major administrative changes at the Lambs Farm may trace to October 14, 1971, when Corinne Owen had the accident that, because of her continuing disability, in her words, "would make me a Lamb myself." Although she was back at the Farm by Christmas, recovery would take at least eighteen months. Her back would never fully recover and her memory would be left with gaps.

The accident prompted a mild personality change. "I was afraid to go out," she recalled. "I found myself talking nasty. I began to throw things out that I really wanted to keep." Her friends became concerned. Longtime Lambs, many of whom view Corinne as a mother, mark the accident as a personal tragedy in their lives.

It was a difficult period. Bob would force Corinne out of her home by telling her that he and her friends were taking her to the Country Inn. Instead, they would drive her to Millie's Pancake House, a great distance from the Lambs Farm. ("I didn't tell you *which* country inn," Bob would say to her when they got there.) Other friends took her to entertainments such as Pheasant Run, a nearby dinner-theater complex.

Corinne's absence from the property and her inability to work as she had—often seven days a week—seemed to bring into focus a growing management problem. Corinne and Bob were hands-on people. Visitors to the Lambs Farm often found Corinne in the silk-screen shop or Bob driving the commuter bus to the train station. By 1971, however, the Lambs' community had grown to between thirty-five and forty members. Bob and Corinne both recognized that better organization was needed. But they still lacked funds. The movement for such change was often, of necessity, on a back burner.

"We never wanted to run the place," Bob said. "From the very start, we wanted to work with our retarded adults. We wanted the board to run things." At that time, however, not even the board was operating as a unit. "They were more like individuals," one observer said. "They contributed work and wisdom and wealth, but not as a unit."

Bob and Corinne had been able to hold the the institution together by dint of incredibly hard work and strong personalities. Each had a patient and supportive spouse who not only bore the burden of caring for the household but also contributed a great deal of time to the Lambs. However, three dozen Lambs, a pet shop, restaurant, gift shop, and the other activities were bound to strain any structure.

One longtime board member observed, "We were growing, too. The board was trying to learn as it went along. We made some mistakes."

The ingredients of transition began as far back as October 1961 when the Illinois Council for the Mentally Retarded issued a letter to all agencies and to the media. It informed its readers that the Lambs Pet Store, which had barely opened, was "not endorsed" by the council. Without actually saying so, the letter hinted that Bob and Corinne were exploiting retarded people—an interesting charge in view of the fact that both had to continue working at outside employment in order to support their families. The letter formed the two sides: a single-minded bureaucracy versus two fiercely independent thinkers. Relations with outside agencies would be strained for at least a decade.

In the years that followed, the gap widened even more. Bob and Corinne simply went their way, carrying out their vision for treatment of retarded adults. The agencies changed, too. Many of the ideas initiated at the Lambs Farm were also introduced in other agencies. Progress was slower for these larger agencies, however. They had to cope with the bureaucracy, the slowness in getting funding, and the fact that some other agencies could not be as selective as the Lambs Farm in their admissions policies.

It was time, however, to bridge the gap. "We needed to improve relations with the state even if no money came in from them," Bob said.

Most board members agreed. The board, after all, was responsible for the operation's fiscal condition—and funds were extremely precarious. "We had always skated on thin ice, but we had faith," Bob said. But not all board members shared that faith. They felt that it was time to seek some funding from the state and to explore the possibility of professional accreditation.

Bob and Corinne had always turned to professionals for advice. Psychologist Delilah White, for example, had evaluated virtually all potential new Lambs. In the early 1970s, Bob solicited funds for a professional evaluation of the entire operation.

The study, funded by the Stone-Brandel Foundation, faulted the facilities and some aspects of the organizational structure. Again, much of what the study criticized could be blamed on the lack of funds. The study contained nothing that the staff did not know. From the perspective of nearly twenty years, in fact, some points appear to be nitpicking. Basically, the study suggested that it was time to give the institution a more professional structure.

The transition from charismatic to professional leadership was not without pain. Given the personalities involved and the high level of caring both had for their charges, such pain was inevitable.

Bob and Corinne had always pioneered new ideas. During Corinne's recuperation in late 1971, she wrote a pamphlet-sized manual titled *Teaching the Mentally Retarded*. It was a model of simplicity and grace and had the endorsement of

Dr. Karl Menninger. But when she gave it to an educator for evaluation, he said, "You can't publish this, Corinne. It's not even in the textbooks yet." The implication was clear: new ideas must work their way through the academic and professional community before they can be considered valid. While that notion has merit, it sometimes means that new ideas are validated only if they orginate within the traditional community.

Much as Bob and Corinne recognized that another structure was needed, they found the transition troublesome. "I guess I felt that the advocates of professionalism were trying to turn the place into a college campus," Bob recalled. "It seemed to me that the retarded needed love, not professionalism." He cited a personal hero, Jean Vanier, founder of the successful l'Arche communities for retarded adults. "The retarded need space in your heart," Vanier had said during a visit to the Lambs Farm.

At the board level, no real clear sides emerged. But the board members were reluctant to make a change that would hurt Bob and Corinne or, more important, diminish their enormous influence on the philosophy of caring that had made the Lambs Farm a success. "It's just that we needed someone in charge whom we could fire," one board member said. Bob and Corinne agreed.

In the mid-1970s, the board made the change. Bob and Corinne were retained in an active status with reduced roles. Lewis Kranz, a genial former military colonel, was hired as executive director.

Kranz tried—with some success. He was still hobbled, just as Bob and Corinne were, by a lack of money. He resigned in 1980 and was succeeded by Al Hattis, who served for less than a year. During these transitional years, Bob and Corinne's roles gradually evolved to emeritus status. They continued to submit ideas for new approaches to training and to solicit funds. Their office became a place where parents and friends could turn when they had concerns.

"Gerry Friedman was the perfect choice for this place,"

Bob said in 1989. "He has the head of a professional and the heart of a caring person." Gerald V. Friedman came to the Lambs Farm as executive director on September 15, 1981. He brought extensive experience in working with the developmentally disabled, excellent political instincts, a thorough knowledge of the state bureaucracy, and a temperament that could calm troubled waters.

"Except for a few brief attempts to make money in the real world," Friedman said in his self-effacing manner, "I've always been in social service work." After earning his undergraduate degree in psychology at Roosevelt University, he completed a master's degree in public health services. He spent several years in army intelligence during the Korean conflict. Upon discharge, he had difficulty finding employment. The job market was glutted with returning veterans. He took a job with Chicago's welfare department as a field representative and shortly after became a caseworker.

In the 1950s, the vocational rehabilitation department ran a large sheltered workshop at Washington and Ada streets—one that made Ping Pong paddles for a large distributor. People on welfare were evaluated and assigned to the workshop. Friedman became a vocational counselor in the workshop. He found that he liked what he was doing. He held a variety of posts at rehab for the next fourteen years.

Friedman then went to work for the Chicago Association of Retarded Citizens, where he was deputy executive director for a dozen years. The agency served some 1,400 clients in schools, sheltered workshops, and apartments. The rehabilitation and sheltered-workshop experience was an ideal preparation for the Lambs Farm.

When Friedman arrived at the Lambs Farm, the management issues were still not settled. "Bob and Corinne's participation—their usefulness—had come into question," he recalled. "There was some confusion about their reduced roles."

"I had heard about them but had never met them," he continued. "I was introduced to them and found them delightful. Some of my colleagues had described them as reli-

gious nuts. I found them to be religious but not nuts. We got
to be friends. I opposed any steps that would separate them
from the Lambs. They are a resource not to be found in
other agencies. It was a rare opportunity to continue their
usefulness."

Friedman brought structure to the operation. He gave
cohesion to its disparate parts. He also had the opportunity
to expose some of the myths about the Lambs Farm. "I had
heard it was only for rich people's families," he said. "Instead, when I got here, I found that there were at least fifty
people who had no families at all or were abject indigents. In
fact, when I came here in September of that year [1981], I
found out that we couldn't even make the November pay-
roll."

In less than ten years, Friedman virtually erased the negative image of the Lambs Farm that had been held by some
professional agencies. "Now if someone has something dis-
paraging to say about the Lambs, they say it behind my
back," he said. "We are held in high regard by all the funders
and, if not all the providers, at least most of them. I think
Bob and Corinne's resentment is well placed. They were
discredited. But parents find this place a paradise even if we
are a countertrend."

The reference to a countertrend has to do with the policy
of not linking Lambs up to services. It means that the Lambs
Farm has resisted trends that its founders believe would be
counterproductive. Their institutional philosophy still objects to the "administration knows best" approach to handling their members. This translates into moving developmentally disabled people from environments such as the
Lambs Farm into private housing.

"When you're planning someone else's life, you've got to
take a lot of other things into account," Friedman said. "You
need to take into account security, warmth, love, and happiness and all the rest of that. This is a community, and the
people who live here are entitled to have a community. We
can't just put them out on the streets, where they can become victims again."

Friedman maintains that the field of retardation is a large one with many approaches to treatment. He bristles at the ideologues in the profession who focus on one way to do something and insist that their method be a remedy for all.

In retrospect, Gerry Friedman acknowledges that Bob and Corinne were ahead of their time. "I'm not certain that retarded people had an affinity for animals," he said, "but what Bob and Corinne discovered was that, if you charged people with responsibility, they would respond to that responsibility. If you told them that they had to get down to the store at 7:30 in the morning or else some animals could die, they did it. This is a concept that other institutions knew for twenty-five or thirty years but didn't come into. That's a long time to wait. Bob and Corinne made that same discovery thirty years ago and put it into practice.

"This field does have its ideologues, and sadly most of the ideologues are not people who deliver service," he continued. "They never had to treat a person. They never had to sit down and have a cup of coffee with a retarded person."

Friedman underlined the often-repeated observation that people who work at the Lambs Farm get very much involved with the people for whom they care. "It happens so frequently that you have to recognize it for what it is," he said. "There's a certain chemistry that takes place within the relationship that endears them to one another. It goes beyond just the job itself." Friedman doesn't expect that every employee will become emotionally involved with the members of the Lambs' community, but he counts such involvement as a plus.

Businesses start slowly at the Lambs Farm. The only exception has been the miniature-golf course, which has been successful from the start. Friedman still has to maintain the delicate balance between considerations of the Lambs' needs and the realities of turning an adequate profit in the many endeavors. Further, there is the state, which now provides 8.3 percent of the Lambs Farm's income. "They provide us with the money, so we have to send them back some paper," he said with calm resignation.

The Lambs' parents have no real legal responsibilities toward their children after they are eighteen, unless the parents have petitioned for guardianship. Some parents do ask for guardianship, but the majority do not. Retardation does not preclude competency. Most of the Lambs, then, are judged to be competent. But parents are generous in supporting their adult children and in promoting the work of the Lambs Farm.

Some time after Friedman came to the Lambs Farm, he set up a program for other clients of the state to receive training in restaurant work, grounds keeping, even work in the personnel office.

State funding for the Lambs Farm comes largely through the Department of Rehabilitation Services (DORS). (The change represents something of an irony: the Lambs Farm now receives financial help for programs the organization was once soundly condemned for providing.) The DORS program does represent growth for the state and for the Lambs Farm. Staff at the Farm can not only train the DORS participants but can also place them in jobs in the community rather than back into a sheltered workshop.

Thanks to the Lambs Farm's excellent placement, training, and workshop programs, the business community has an increasing relationship with the Farm. "Businesspeople will give us a first shot out of a measure of sympathy for what we're trying to do," Friedman said. "But we've got to perform or they won't give us a second shot. We've got to be as good as anyone else."

The Lambs Farm now employs 130 people to support 180. The numbers, which suggest almost intensive care, are high because three shifts are required in some areas. But the big staff is needed largely because employees work alongside the Lambs in all the retail operations.

"Without Gerry Friedman, this place would have closed down," Bob Terese said. Clearly, Friedman provided the link the Lambs Farm's leaders were seeking. He has combined professional experience with entrepreneurial gifts that brought the organization into the 1980s. Bob and Corinne continue to cultivate support for the Lambs Farm and to bring a personal touch to its complex operations. The combination has made the Lambs of Libertyville one of the best-known care-giving institutions in the greater Chicago area.

Today, the certificates on the wall proclaim the organization's full accreditation by the Commission on Accreditation of Rehabilitation Services for its programs in vocational evaluation, occupational skills therapy, job placement, and work, activity, and residential services.

Although the transition from founders' management to professional management was slow and difficult, what has emerged is an institution with both a head and a heart.

◆ Lambs Tales ◆
"Ben"

Don't ask a developmentally disabled person a question unless you are prepared for an honest answer. Retarded people are capable of ducking a question, but they rarely do. Some, indeed, seem incapable of it. Emotionally, most have healthy egos and good self-esteem. With proper support, they grow to accept themselves as they are and live comfortably within the limits of their disability. They are unaffected, unfiltered, unvarnished. That is their charm.

"Ben" has Down's syndrome. He is a resident at the Lambs Farm but spends many weekends with his parents.

When he arrived home one weekend, he appeared depressed. His parents probed gently: "Do you have a problem, Ben?"

"Yes."

"Do you want to talk about it?"

"No."

"Is there someone you'd like to talk to?"

"Uncle Steve."

"That's fine. We'll call him. But, Ben, we're your parents. You can talk to us."

"I know. But what if you're the problem?"

♦ Chapter 12 ♦

The Future

J. Curtis Jones is president of the John Morton Co., a group of thirty-five marketing consultants who provide marketing strategies, largely to high-tech corporations, in the United States and Europe. His wife, Phyllis, is an attorney who does substantial work on legislation involving the mentally handicapped. Their son, Peter, is brain damaged. He has been a member of the Lambs' community since 1987.

"Peter was slow in sitting up," Curt said. "At six to nine months, we noticed a balance problem. Later, there was a speech problem. We took him to Michael Reese Hospital for diagnosis, and we were informed that he was brain damaged."

Peter Jones is like many other Lambs. They learn to compensate for their disabilities. He is clever at finding ways to say things that help to bypass his speech impediment, and he has a very positive personality, very tenacious. Now in his midtwenties, he commutes daily to the Lambs Sheltered Workshop, nicknamed "Wire City" by the Lambs, although no one is quite sure why. Someday, he will become a resident at the Lambs Farm. For now, however, he enjoys living with his parents and his sister in their Winnetka home.

Peter Jones's family is more affluent than the majority of Lambs-related families. But in every other way, the Joneses endured all the problems of raising a handicapped child in a world that is geared to the successful child: the honor roll student, the football captain, and the pretty cheerleader.

Although their upper-class suburb offered a cooperative program for children with special needs, the Joneses experienced insensitive and entrenched bureaucracies that often placed the politics of the system over the needs of the impaired children.

The pattern of anxious parents versus the health professionals may seem like a stereotype. However, the number of times it has been found suggests that there is some merit in parental disappointment and anger. The reasons for this pattern are difficult to trace. They may stem from the lingering belief that mentally handicapped people cannot be helped, that they can only receive basic skill training and endure custodial care.

A number of professionals at other institutions sympathized with the parental anger but were at a loss to find a completely satisfactory answer. One observer likened the situation to that of a nursing home for the elderly: "There are so many rules, so many codes, so many procedures that those who run nursing homes must live up to. Each of the rules makes a measure of sense, but taken altogether, they amount to another form of neglect." Furthermore, the developmentally disabled display a complex variety of problems. Treating the disabled individually can be very difficult.

In 1982, Curt Jones became a member of the board of directors of the Lambs Farm. He served on a number of its committees and, in 1989, was named to a two-year term as president of the board.

"It's the best board I've ever seen," Bob Terese said. (He and Corinne attend all board meetings.) Jack Stein, immediate past president and board member since 1977, agreed. "Now we know what we're looking for," he said. "We've gone through a lot. We had a lot of start-up problems. There were problems with unqualified administrators. But we didn't know any better. We were learning, too."

"Now we're in a better financial situation," Stein continued. "Now we've got a good professional staff. Now we've got a lot to be pleased with." Stein has served on virtually every committee of the board. He still serves on the nominating, business, development and public relations, and long-range planning committees.

Jones agrees with Stein. "We're now a mature organization," he said. "We're helped by the fact that there is little concern about pride of authorship in the things we do. I think we get that from the Lambs themselves."

In mid-1989, the administration and board of the Lambs Farm developed a plan that would spell out the strategies for the next decade. The plan called for improved promotion of the organization's businesses and for communications with parents and local industry. After over twenty-five years, the Lambs are still emerging from what one observer called the "gunslinging" early days when numbers were small and risks easier to control.

Those who now monitor the mission of the Lambs Farm will never permit profitability to take precedence over the mission "to enrich the quality of the Lambs' lives and to maximize their life skills and experiences at home, at work, and in the community." Yet it is clear that the businesses must produce more profits if the community is to remain viable. The board has charged the business committee with the task of improving profitability through new ventures, more extensive advertising, investigation of more wholesale marketing, and increased business at the Country Inn.

The approach has tightened guidelines but hasn't diminished the earlier spirit. While watching the bottom line, the board approved the purchase of a full-blown amusement park train that will be installed on the property in 1990–1991. Board members remain willing to find new challenges for the Lambs.

Fund-raising efforts produce about 30 percent of the Lambs Farm's revenues. The strategic plan directs that more efforts be made in the area of deferred giving—wills, trusts, and the like. Parents with the means are also being asked to consider establishing trust funds that will provide for their son or daughter. The Lambs Care Trust has been established to meet this need.

At present, the original fifty-one acres are nearly fully utilized or planned for utilization. The twelve new acres acquired in the late 1970s remain unused, but through the courtesy of Holabird & Root, a prominent Chicago architectural firm, the Lambs Farm now has a land-use plan that will guide future planning.

"The Founders' Building is our most immediate project," Curt Jones said. Budgeted at $1.2 million, it will answer the need for a year-round recreation and learning center and will provide space for administrative offices. Until late 1990, the administration was housed in the basement of the first residence, completed in 1976. According to the strategic plan, the administrators "have become increasingly cramped with declining utility and efficiency."

The Founders' Building was made possible through a matching gift of $600,000 from a donor who remains anonymous. Ground was broken in early 1990.

Additional off-site community living remains another goal, especially for the higher-functioning Lambs. "I love it here," one of them said. "I don't want to lose my connection. I'll always need help with some things, but I would like to live in a separate community with some other Lambs like myself. I'd like to be able to go shopping on my own—just things like that."

Currently, the Lambs Farm owns a single-family home in Waukegan that provides off-site community living for four residents. More such homes are contemplated for the future.

The Lambs are getting older. Original members of the community, then only in their late teens, are now in their midforties. A few have entered their sixties. There has been much discussion about establishing a geriatric program and residence. Without such a residence, located on or off the present property, most Lambs would be seriously compromised. Some have no family and little financial means. Others enjoy some income but would find it virtually impossible to obtain entrance to another facility. Discussions have already begun to initiate a geriatric program that will address housing, vocational alternatives, recreation, and medical needs. The board hopes to have a geriatric program residence in place by 1995.

Like every not-for-profit organization, the Lambs Farm relies on contributions. Proposed tax legislation could reduce or eliminate the existing tax deduction for charitable contributions. The Lambs Farm must therefore budget against possible declines in income. Further, cuts in the federal government's budget in the past ten years have significantly increased competition for contributed dollars.

In the near future, the Lambs Farm will establish an endowment fund. For thirty years, the organization has had to use every contributed dollar for immediate needs. It now seeks to have a fund, conceptually akin to the endowment fund at universities, that will supply continuous income. Some monies have already been received.

In addition, the Lambs Farm, in common with all such facilities, must monitor legislation that affects the welfare of the Lambs. The Chafee bill, for example, introduced by Republican Senator John H. Chafee of Rhode Island, would severely limit the number of residents housed in an Intermediate Care Facility. However well intentioned, passage of such a bill would virtually close the "dorm" at the Lambs Farm, even though it provides high-level care for all its residents.

Like any organizational study, the strategic plan for the Lambs Farm contains a summary of the community's strengths and weaknesses. Listed among the strengths were the names Corinne Owen and Bob Terese. Among the identified weaknesses was an even more poignant note: "The age of the Founders—No replacement for them."

Epilogue

On June 9, 1989, over 550 parents and friends—the largest crowd ever to attend the Good Shepherd Award Dinner—gathered at the Lambs Farm to salute the co-founders. The dinner, initiated in 1969, is held only every three years because Bob and Corinne "didn't want to overdo the solicitation."

The dinner is held under colorfully striped tents at the Country Inn. Although tickets are $125 each, it is not touted primarily as a fund-raising event. It is rather an appreciation dinner, and in 1989, the Lambs were paying tribute to their greatest benefactors.

At the first dinner, their good friend, Dr. Karl Menninger, received the Good Shepherd Award, which is given to exceptional humanitarians who have looked beyond their own concerns to the needs of others. In the dinners that followed, the Lambs honored W. Clement Stone, who had provided the property; Clinton E. Frank, the publicist who had contributed so many services; Betty Ford, who had visited the Lambs twice; Mr. and Mrs. Gaylord Donnelly, James S. Kemper, and Joseph Regenstein, Jr.—all successful Chicago businesspeople and philanthropists.

Now the coveted award was given to a man who encountered his first retarded person while driving a bus and a woman who came to a school for the retarded because she needed a job. Bob thought that he could teach them some simple exercises; Corinne believed she could teach them something about the seasons of the year. Together, they made history.

No serious study of the history of the development of facilities for the mentally handicapped could be written to-day without reference to the Lambs Farm. Professionals from virtually every state and over forty foreign countries have visited the Farm. Successful Lambs-like efforts have been undertaken in other states.

Bob and Corinne have often been asked about "franchis-ing" the concept and opening other facilities. They have repeatedly and firmly declined. "Let them come and take whatever ideas they can find here. We're happy to share them. And, God knows, there's a need. But we just wanted to do this. We didn't want anything that would take us away from our special people."

Chicago radio personality Bob Collins acted as master of ceremonies at the 1989 dinner. The keynote address was given by Chicago Bears coach Mike Ditka, a member of the Pro Football Hall of Fame, Coach of the Year, and Super Bowl winner. There was the usual standing ovation.

The entire evening would have warmed anyone's heart. Bob and Corinne were moved beyond words. The dinner was a validation of all that they believed. Most likely, Bob and Corinne were touched more than anything else by the fact that one of their Lambs gave the invocation and many others served as greeters and table hosts.

In nearly thirty years, Bob Terese and Corinne Owen had taught a huge urban and suburban community that fear is a great barrier in society. The mentally retarded were afraid of normal people, and normal people were afraid of them. They opened a pet store and began breaking down fears. They broke through barriers of suspicion and replaced them with love and respect. "Corinne and I had faith that society, if given the opportunity to meet the mentally retarded in a positive way, would appreciate their gentle qualities. And we were right," he told the audience.

They had been honored before. The Alexian Brothers Medical Center had presented them with the Modern Samaritan Award; the Protestant Foundation of Greater Chicago and the Caritas Society had honored them. Corinne received Loyola University's Camelia Award and in 1990 was given an honorary doctorate by her alma mater, North Park College. De Paul University gave its Distinguished Alumni Award to Bob.

However, now the Lambs themselves were honoring their founders. "Tonight," Corinne said, "is the high point of my life!"

Months after the dinner, Corinne Owen sat with friends in her West Chicago home. Her dining room table was stacked with immense scrapbooks in which she had carefully preserved the record of the birth and growth of the Lambs' community.

She turned the pages as if viewing them for the first time. Her enthusiasm was undiminished. Although her 1971 accident had affected her short-term memory, her memory for the incidents that marked turning points in the development of the community was precise. Above all, she knew names. Her carefully preserved archives are a story of faith, love, and hard work.

Corinne Owen and Bob Terese have achieved a revered status. They are at their offices each day, writing letters, making calls, helping the development office find new avenues of funds, and promoting the work of the Lambs.

Not long after the Good Shepherd Award Dinner, some visitors were guests at House Three at the Farm. Following dinner, Michelle Hendrickson, a member of the community for ten years, capsulized everything that the Lambs Farm represents: "I go away from this place to visit my family or for some other reason. But when I return and see that Lambs sign on the barn, I know I'm home! There's no place like home."